MW01613547

Letters
TO MY
FANS

PUBLISHED BY

TWI, Inc.
P.O., Box 888
Hermitage, TN 37076

Art direction and design: Kim Russell / Wahoo Designs

Library of Congress Control Number: Applied for.

ISBN: 978-0-9825887-0-3

Printed in the U.S.A.

IN LOVING MEMORY OF

JEAN BROWN

My fan club president for 25-years, and the
best fan anyone could ever
be lucky enough to have.

OTHER BOOKS BY BILL ANDERSON

Whisperin' Bill - An Autobiography

I Hope You're Living As High On The Hog As The Pig You Turned Out To Be

BILL ANDERSON

Letters

TO MY

FANS

VOLUME ONE   2003-2006

CONTENTS

INTRODUCTION

A long time before I was a country music songwriter, singer, television personality, or any version or extension thereof, I was a country music fan.

I grew up in South Carolina and Georgia idolizing my favorite country singers, be they local radio performers or nationally known stars. My two favorites were Byron Parker, who sang with his band, The Hillbillies, on WIS Radio in Columbia, and Hank Williams who sang on The Grand Ole Opry from Nashville. I loved the music they made, identified with its plaintive, simple messages, and went out of my way to study, research, and learn as much about each of them as I could.

In my early teenage years, I wanted nothing more than to own every single recording Hank Williams had ever made, so I decided one day to write him a fan letter. It was crude, I'm sure, written as best as I remember in pencil on a half sheet of lined notebook paper. It said something like, "Dear Mr. Williams…I am a big fan of yours and I would like to have a list of every record you have made so I can be sure I have them all in my collection." Nothing much fancier than that I know.

I put the note on top of my Daddy's chest of drawers in his bedroom and asked him to mail it to Hank Williams, %WSM Radio, Nashville, Tennessee. He promised he would, and I took him at his word. To this day I don't know for sure if Dad mailed the letter or not. But I do know for sure that I never received a reply from Hank Williams. And I was crushed.

I watched the mailbox every day for weeks, just knowing I'd get a letter from him. Or, if not a personal letter, at least that list of his recordings that I so badly wanted. When it didn't come and it didn't come, I was hurt. Eventually I grew angry. Hurt and anger can sometimes form an unhealthy combination.

One day, in what surely qualifies as one of the dumbest, most thoughtless moments of my life, I decided to wipe Hank Williams off my radar screen forever. I gathered up every single 78rpm recording of his that I possessed....and it was a large stack, recordings he made as Hank Williams and those he released under the pseudonym of Luke the Drifter....and traded them to a schoolmate for all his Spike Jones records. Hank Williams hadn't answered my letter. Who needed him? I decided to laugh at the weird, wacky music of Spike Jones instead of crying when Hank recited the mournful story of "The Funeral."

Eventually, of course, I got over it. And to this day I always put Hank Williams at the top of my list of the songwriters and entertainers who influenced my career. But he influenced me not only by the songs he gave the world, but by the one thing he failed to give a young fan.

Unknowingly, he taught me a lesson that has served me well for over a half-century in the entertainment business: I have gone out of my way all these years to never break anyone's heart like he broke mine. I have tried to answer every fan letter I have ever received.

It hasn't always been easy, and I'm sure I've missed a few. But back in the days before the internet and e-mail, I often stayed up late into the night typing on an old manual typewriter or writing letters by hand. I wrote from hotel rooms on the road, from the front lounges or the rear staterooms on tour busses criss-crossing the country. Now it's on a laptop computer, but the object is still the same. Don't ever disappoint a fan like my hero once disappointed me.

My process seemed to serve me well until the fall of 2003 when my father passed away. I returned home from a tour through western Canada to find over three-thousand e-mails, cards, letters, and expressions of sympathy from country music fans and friends the world over. For the first time in my career, I knew there was no possible way for me to respond to all the mail. It was simply overwhelming.

On October 15th of that year, I went onto my website at www.billanderson.com and composed the first of what has turned out to be hundreds of letters to my fans. As you'll see shortly, it was a simple letter designed to primarily let as many people as possible know how much their thoughtfulness had meant to me in one of the saddest, most agonizing moments of my life.

I didn't realize it at the time, but that one letter triggered my desire to write another one a few days later. Then another....and almost before I knew it I had launched a series of letters that were being read by people from all over the world. And now that series of Letters To My Fans has become the book you are holding in your hand.

Well, it's the first three years of those letters. Later we'll package the letters from the three following years and release them as Volume II in the series. After that, who knows?

In going through these letters in one complete volume, I've noticed they seem to have taken on a new life. They read almost like a diary from three exciting years of my life. You'll relive with me everything from the grief I felt in losing the last of my original family members to the unbridled joy that was mine when I was presented the Country Music Association's Song of the Year award on nationwide television onstage at Madison Square Garden in New York City. I've also managed to throw in a few photos and some lighthearted asides that I trust you will enjoy as well.

I hope you will enjoy sharing these moments with me again...or for the first time...whichever your case may be. And just think: Had ole Hank lived another five decades or so, he might have done it this-a-way himself.

2003

*"Find something you like doing
so much you'd do it for nothing.
Then learn to do it so well, they'll
pay you, and you've got it made."*

October 15, 2003

Hi Folks:

Thanks for visiting our web site. I hope you'll enjoy looking around, and that you'll come back and see us again soon and often.

When I arrived home from my cross-country tour of Canada, I had over 3,000 e-mails offering condolences and sympathy on the death of my father who passed away while I was gone. I cannot begin to tell you how touched I was that so many of you took the time to write and express your sorrow on my behalf.

There is no possible way I could possibly answer all those e-mails personally, so I decided to use our Home page as a way of conveying my appreciation to you all. Thanks so much to those of you who took the time and trouble to write.

To the folks in Brandon, Manitoba; Regina and Saskatoon, Saskatchewan; and Red Deer, Alberta: I'm so sorry I had to cancel my appearances there, but it could not be helped. We are trying very hard to reschedule the dates for a time early next year. Cross your fingers that we'll be able to work it out.

Keep watching this space on our web site as I plan to use it more often to communicate with you. And thanks again for being the greatest fans and friends a guy could ever have.

My best always,

October 23, 2003

Hi Folks:

And welcome to our web site. It's good to have you visiting whether you're a first-timer or if you've been with us many times before.

Many of you have written recently asking why I haven't been on the Grand Ole Opry these past few weeks and wondering, I'm sure, why I have not answered your recent e-mails. It's very simple: I've been on vacation.

I had planned to take some time off following our Canadian tour, and then when my father passed away in late September, I realized I needed the vacation time more than ever. So, I've been up on the coast of Maine these past couple of weeks taking in the gorgeous fall colors and simply relaxing in one of my favorite places. When it started snowing this morning, though, I decided it was time to head back south!!

Following our October 25th concert in Biloxi, Mississippi, I have some family time booked in Georgia before returning to the Opry (at the Ryman!) on Halloween. The following night I'll get to spend my birthday there as well. And then it's headlong into CMA Week, which is one of the busiest (and most exciting) times of the year in Music City.

Thanks for your many continued kindnesses to me. Keep watching this space...I'll be writing more soon. My best to you all.

Jim Anderson

2

November 7, 2003

Hi Folks!

And thanks for stopping by our web site.

Well, the busiest week of the year for the Nashville music industry has come and gone, and as always things were hectic but fun. I want to congratulate all the winners from the various awards presentations. Lots of great folks made lots of great music this past year!

Thanks to Kenny Chesney, producers Buddy Cannon and Norro Wilson, and songwriter-deluxe, Dean Dillon, I got to partake in a couple of awards for co-writing "A Lot Of Things Different." Dean and I won a BMI Citation signifying our song as one of the 50 Most Performed Country Songs of 2003, plus we also received a very special award from the Nashville Songwriters Association International.

The NSAI Award is voted on by other songwriters who cast ballots for the "Ten Songs I Wish I Had Written" each year. There is no greater honor than to be recognized by your peers which makes this award doubly appreciated.

In between all the parties and celebrations, I somehow found time to tape two more of my radio shows for XM Satellite Radio this week. My guests were Charlie Daniels and Janie Fricke. I hope you'll be listening for Bill Anderson Visits With The Legends which airs several times each week on XM Channel 10, America.

I'll be spending a lot of time in the recording studio these next two weeks working on a couple of new album projects. Wish us luck, and be watching for news about our upcoming releases.

Have a great week, and thanks for everything.

November 14, 2003

Hi...

And thanks for stopping by our web site.

As I was looking at the two pictures to your right, it occurred to me that one of my favorite things about performing a concert out on the road somewhere is having the chance to visit with you, my fans and friends, after the concert is over. And I can't begin to tell you how many folks thank us for taking the time to make those visits, and the subsequent autograph and photograph sessions, possible. "So many artists don't sign autographs anymore," they say, and I cringe because I know so many of my friends in the music business would love to sign autographs and meet the fans just like I do.

Johnny Koonce

But when you're playing to packed houses inside 20,000-seat arenas and 50,000-seat stadiums, signing autographs after a show is totally impossible. I'm lucky, though, because most of our venues are smaller and the crowds more manageable, and I get to visit with folks like you see pictured here. The gentleman in the top photo with a copy of my late-seventies album called "Bill" is Johnny Koonce, and he brought that album to our recent show in Biloxi, Mississippi. Why? Because he wrote one of the songs I recorded in that package called "All Together Now (Let's Fall Apart)" and he had never had the opportunity to thank me for recording it. His song, of course, was a much bigger hit by Ronnie Milsap, but it meant a lot to me that Johnny came to our show and asked me to sign my version. The young lady in the bottom picture is named Michelle Wooten, and she is a very special fan whose parents brought her to see our show. She wanted nothing more than to give me a big hug after the show, and the photographer just happened to catch the big grin on my face as it was happening. Both Johnny and Michelle thanked me, but I feel I should have thanked them. They, and folks like them, are, to me, such a large part of what country music is all about.

Michelle Wooten

November 24, 2003

I'M THANKFUL....

For the sun that came up over the Tennessee hills this morning, and that I was able to get up out of bed, make coffee, and be gifted with another day as a small part of God's incredible creation.

I'm thankful for the sound of a crying steel guitar, a lonesome fiddle, and the fact that after all these years I'm still awed by good country songs, good pickin', and good singing.

I'm thankful for the lives and the legacies of those we've lost this year, including Johnny Cash and Don Gibson, who inspired me with their talents and honored me with their friendship. And I'm thankful that Carl Smith (finally!) and Floyd Cramer received their just due by being inducted into the Country Music Hall of Fame.

I'm thankful for the memories of Roger Miller, Grandpa Jones, Stringbean, Jimmy Gateley and Lewis Grizzard. Hardly a day goes by but what I don't remember something one of them said or did, and it never fails to make me smile. (I'm even thankful Jimmy Dean has my home telephone number, because just the sound of his voice on the line can make me burst out laughing!)

I'm thankful that my dad lived for over ninety-two years, and died so peacefully, simply sitting in the living room in his favorite chair. And I'm thankful for the double headstone in the little cemetery in Georgia that assures me he and Mama are once again sleeping side by side as they should be.

I'm thankful for parents who took the time when I was a child to teach me about the word of God. I sleep better at night resting in His promise that someday I'll see my loved ones again.

I'm thankful for a sister whose cancer is apparently in remission, and thankful for the peace she has found through her struggles. I'm even

5

thankful for my own adversities, because in many ways they have served to re-introduce me to myself.

I'm thankful every time I hear my son's voice on the other end of the telephone line, because I know he's landed another airplane safely and delivered his passengers securely to their destination.

I'm thankful for three children and four grandchildren who love me, not because of who I am but in spite of it. I'm thankful that they want to spend part of their Thanksgiving holiday with me, and I'm thankful that they allow me to spend mine with them.

I'm thankful for our servicemen and women who, by no choice of their own, must spend Thanksgiving apart from their friends and families this year because they are somewhere helping protect the freedoms the rest of us too often take for granted.

And I'm thankful for each of you, my fans and my friends, who stopped by my web site today. May your Thanksgiving holiday be blessed, and may you spend it with the ones you love.

All professional songwriters receive unsolicited material from amateur writers. Some push the limits of creativity. Don Sampson once received one called, "Even Cockatiels Get The Blues."

A man came up to me following a show in Pennsylvania and asked, "When you made the recording with Roy Acuff, was he still alive?"

6

December 1, 2003

You don't have to have known me very long or know me very well to have picked up on the fact that I am a sports junkie. I keep up with just about every sport there is, but my true passions are...and have always been...baseball and football.

Until the Houston Oilers moved to Nashville and became the Tennessee Titans, however, my primary interest in football was on the high school and college level. I liked the professional game, but I never developed a passion for it until "we" got "our" team. Now I schedule my tours around the Titans' home games (drives my booking agent crazy!), and I'm there and in my seat every time they kick off at the Coliseum. I've watched every road game on TV this season, except for the two I traveled to and saw in person!

But I also happen to like another Nashville product called country music. I guess that's why a letter to the editor that appeared Sunday in our local newspaper, The Tennessean, bothered me. The letter said, in essence, that the "Welcome To Nashville" road signs at our city limits should be rewritten so that they no longer read, "Home Of The Grand Ole Opry" but read instead, "Home Of The Tennessee Titans."

I won't bore you with the details, but I had something to do with the "Home Of The Grand Ole Opry" signs being placed at the Nashville city limits in the first place. It wasn't easy to coax the city fathers into putting those signs up back in the early sixties, and I don't want to see them disappear. Not even to be replaced by recognition of the football team that I enjoy so much.

I look at it this way: There are thirty-one other cities across America that could announce at the limits of their cities that they are the home of such-and-such professional football team. But there is only one city in this great country of ours that can claim to be the home of something as wonderful and uniquely American as the Grand Ole Opry. I tell people all the time that you don't have to be a country music fan to appreciate what the Opry is and what it stands for any more than you have to be a horse-racing fan to appreciate the Kentucky Derby or an auto-racing fan to appreciate the Indianapolis 500. The Derby and the Indy 500 are special slices of Americana, and their home cities proudly proclaim their existence at every conceivable opportunity as well they should. But those races are only run once a year...the Titans play but eight regular season games in Nashville each season...while the Grand Ole Opry is staged a minimum of three times a week, is seen and heard and revered by millions of fans around the globe, and it has been for over seventy-eight years! Let's fill the stadium every time the Titans take the field. Let's throw them the biggest parade in the history of the city when they win the Super Bowl, but let's leave the road signs alone. "Welcome To Nashville - Home Of The Grand Ole Opry." Sure, I'm prejudiced, but it's got a great ring to it. Plus, no other city can make that statement!

A reporter recently asked Jan Howard if she was bitter because her records weren't being played on mainstream country radio anymore. She replied, "No, I'm not bitter. I'm too busy being thankful."

METROPOLITAN NASHVILLE
DAVIDSON COUNTY

HOME OF
THE GRAND OLE OPRY

December 5, 2003

For the past couple of years I have been hosting a weekly show on XM Satellite Radio called "Bill Anderson Visits With The Legends."
The show is exactly what the title implies: I have some of the great country music legends come by the studio, and we just turn on the microphones and visit with each other. The shows are not interviews, they are not scripted in any way, they are just conversations between country music folks with a lot of laughter and a bit of music, both recorded and live, thrown in for good measure.
I know some of you have XM radios and you've heard the programs, but I'm aware that most of you probably do not and have not. That's why I'm so excited about what XM has decided to do:
They are making three of our most outstanding programs available to you on compact discs just in time for Christmas!
My guests on this special 3-CD pack are Merle Haggard, Willie Nelson, and The Oak Ridge Boys! When you order, you'll get over three hours of conversation, music, laughter, and memories from three of the greatest acts in the history of country music. And you can keep the CDs and play them over and over again. I really think you'll enjoy them, and they make wonderful gifts as well.
There is a toll-free number you can call to check it out…
1-800-XXX-XXXX. Or you can click here to visit the website.
People write me every week from all across the country saying that they learn new things about each artist we visit with when they listen to our shows. And they love the musical journeys back across the years as well. These CD's* are truly treasures, and for just $23.99 they are yours to keep forever. I hope you'll check them out, and I hope you'll enjoy listening to them as much as we enjoyed making them for you.
If you're a true country music fan, I predict you will!

* these CDs are not available anymore.

December 22, 2003

I accepted the fact early on in my career that show business is not a Monday through Friday, nine-to-five job. An entertainer doesn't usually get weekends and holidays off like "normal" folks. I don't ever remember being home for a 4th of July celebration, and I've been on the road many times at Thanksgiving, New Years, Easter, Mother's Day, Father's Day, and Groundhog Day. And, to be honest, I've complained about it a time or two over the years.

But now I'm beginning to realize that in these days of extended families, fractured families, and varied lifestyles, we traveling minstrels aren't the only ones who have to adjust our schedules come holiday time.

A friend called Thursday night to tell me he and his family were headed to Indiana to "spend Christmas" with his parents and siblings. I double-checked the calendar, and "Christmas" isn't until December 25th. He was going a tad early, wasn't he? He said it was the only way he could fit a visit with his family into a schedule that also included spending time with his wife's parents, both sets of grandparents, her children from a previous marriage, and various other kinfolks scattered around the country.

My son is an airline pilot, and being young and perched on one of the lower rungs of the corporate ladder, he has to fly on Christmas Day this year. So, our family will celebrate Christmas on Saturday the 27th when he has landed safely at home.

I'm not sure this is all bad. Christmas is a "day", of course, but it's also a "season" and a "spirit." How many times have we all heard, "I wish the Christmas spirit could last all year long." Well, maybe it can. At least nowadays it can extend from a week or two prior to December 25th until who-knows how much later. I know military families who aren't planning to unwrap their gifts until loved ones come home in February and March.

Whenever and wherever and however you celebrate this holiday season, may it be a warm and wonderful time...and on whatever day your holiday arrives, may you be fortunate enough to spend it with the ones you love.

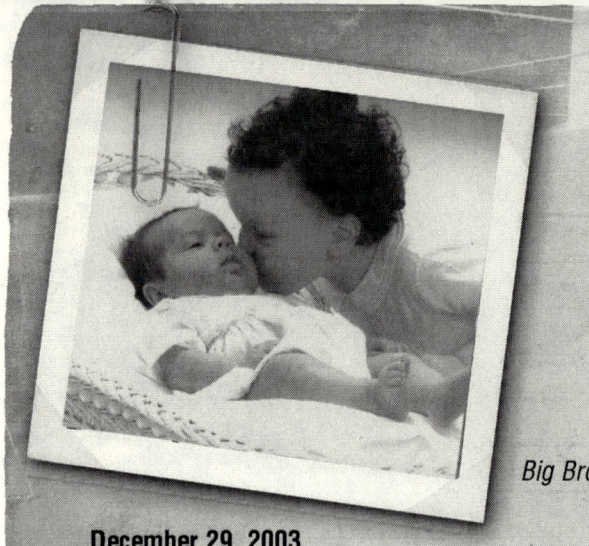

Big Brother...meet Little Brother

December 29, 2003

My 14-month old grandson, Blake, came to our family Christmas gathering wearing a tiny sweatshirt with a picture of a young boy playing baseball and the words, "I'm The Big Brother," emblazoned across the front.

In all the excitement of the day, I didn't pay much attention to the shirt at first. I knew there was a charitable organization in Nashville called the Big Brothers, and I figured Blake's mom and dad had made a Christmastime contribution to the charity and perhaps gotten the shirt in return.

It wasn't until Jamey and Beth finally picked Blake up, held him almost in my face, and confronted me with, "Hey, read his shirt!" that I realized I was being told there's a new little Anderson on the way!

I haven't been quite as blind to the approaching New Year as I was to the approaching new baby. In many ways, I've been ready for 2004 ever since early 2003.

The arrival of a new year, like the impending arrival of a new baby, provides us all with an opportunity to wipe the slates clean...to put our past mistakes and failures behind us...and to begin anew. My wish for you and for me is that we're able to move beyond the disappointments, failures, and sadness of last year and into the new year with renewed determination, hope, and optimism.

In my case, I have to. I'm gonna have a new little grandbaby looking up to me come August!

Happy New Year!

2004

January 6, 2004

I learned a painful lesson over the holidays.

Like many of you, I'm sure, I have always seemed to function best by writing notes to myself reminding me to do things. Whether it's a loaf of bread I need to remember to pick up at the store or a business associate I need to telephone, I'll come a lot closer to remembering it if I simply jot it down on a sheet of paper.

Just before the holidays, I wrote two notes to myself, laid them on my desk, and didn't rediscover them until it was too late. Each note was a reminder to call an old friend. This almost seems surreal now, but the names I had written were Dave Dudley and Vestal Goodman.

I had gotten a new phone number on Dave, and wanted to call and invite him to be a guest on my "Visit With The Legends" radio show next time he was in Nashville. XM satellite radio reaches a large segment of the truck driving population, and what country singer spoke to the truckers through his music better than Dave Dudley? Sadly, Dave died of a heart attack December 22nd.

I had wanted to speak with Vestal Goodman for two reasons. First, just the sound of her voice always made me feel better. She was an up-beat, spiritual woman, and like everyone else in our business, I loved her a lot. The second reason I wanted to talk with her was to issue an invitation for her to appear on our upcoming City Lights Festival this June down in Commerce, Georgia. I know she would have donated her time and been with us had she been able to fit it into her schedule. But Vestal died of complications from the flu on December 27th.

The two notes were still lying on my desk the morning I went back to my office after Christmas. I still haven't thrown them away. In them lies a great lesson: We should never postpone getting in touch with those who are special in our lives.

I'd give anything to hear Vestal's cheerful, "Well, hi darlin'!" ringing in my ear one more time. And Dave's rich baritone teasing me for the millionth time about the morning I stood outdoors in a blinding Canadian snowstorm and tried to sell him a luggage trailer.

But I waited too long to call. And I'll be sorry for the rest of my life.

14

January 9, 2004

I want to thank the folks at Country Weekly magazine, and associate editor, Larry Holden, in particular, for the very nice article they wrote and published about me in their January 20th issue. (It's the one with Tim & Faith on the bright yellow cover in case you missed it and might like to stop reading this right now and run out and pick up a copy!) I wonder if the general public realizes the gamble an entertainer, a politician, or even a business person takes every time they grant an interview to a newspaper or a magazine. A writer, by what he or she writes or doesn't write, can make the interviewee look smart or stupid, successful or unsuccessful, and can help or hinder the reader's perception of that person and his or her career. Consider the following two mythical sentences. One shows the entertainer in a positive light, the other not so positive:

"Joe Smith's new album, which has been out for only four weeks, has already sold over 90,000 copies!" Sounds pretty impressive, huh? The writer shows ole Joe in a pretty favorable light. But say another writer, with the same set of facts in front of him, has an ax to grind with Joe. So he writes, "Joe Smith's new album has been out for a month already and hasn't even sold 100,000 copies."

Did both writers tell the truth? Yes. Did either writer lie? No. Is Joe Smith going to appreciate one writer's work more than the other's? You're darned right he is. Did he have any control over what was written by either writer? None whatsoever.

The press, by and large, has been extremely good to me over the years, and I appreciate it. And I particularly appreciate it when a fine writer like Larry Holden and a publication like Country Weekly go out of their way to present us veterans of country music in a favorable light. Thanks, gang. It's a great way to start off a new year!

January 19, 2004

My sister, Mary, and I are at the beginning of the long, arduous, and sometimes painful process of settling our parents' estate. On many days it's not a lot of fun. On the other hand, Mom and Dad always told us not to be sad when they died. "We've had full, wonderful lives," they would say, "and we want you to remember the good times. Laugh at them every chance you get."

Well, obedient children that we've always been, we are doing just that. Today Mary reminded me of the time Dad bought Mom a book on improving her memory by word association. They traveled a lot in connection with his work, and Dad said he wished Mom would try harder to remember the names of the people they met along the way. Dad never forgot a name in his life. Mom, on the other hand, seldom remembered one.

So Dad bought the book, Mom read the book, and off they went to a business meeting somewhere. The first night they were there, they were introduced to a Mr. and Mrs. Westinghouse. Mom very politely called them by name, and Dad had to have been pleased. They didn't see the Westinghouse's again until several days later at which time Mom spotted Mrs. Westinghouse across the hotel lobby. Hoping to impress Dad with her new and improved memory, she rushed over and said, "Well, hello again, Mrs. Refrigerator!"

Dad never bought Mom any more books. But they would both be laughing right along with us now at the retelling of this story. They didn't have a lot in the way of material possessions, but they left us a treasure chest of marvelous memories. I hope I can do as well by my children someday.

Lib & Jim Anderson

January 24, 2004

Soap opera stars do it. Professional athletes do it. Polka musicians, jazz musicians, blues singers and musicians do it. Even gospel singers have been known to do it. But does anybody have more fun doing it than the stars of the Grand Ole Opry? I doubt it.

Even while you're reading this we're doing it...cruising with our fans and friends in the sparkling waters and warm sunshine of the western Caribbean.

I've lost count of how many Grand Ole Opry cruises I've been on, but each one is a special and unique experience unto itself. We eat, we lie in the sun, we eat, we play music, we eat, we visit wonderful ports of call, and did I mention that we eat? I have a ritual when I return home from an Opry cruise: First, I hide my bathroom scales. Second, I take my clothes to the alterations lady. Third, I promise to never visit another midnight buffet as long as I live!

I just wish each and every person who reads this could someday go with us on an Opry cruise. If you're a country music fan, there's simply no better place to be. There's a live Opry show on stage every night, followed by an invitation-only cocktail party with the stars. During the day there are autograph sessions and picture-taking opportunities galore.....kinda like Fan Fair on board an ocean liner. Heck, I'm already excited about next year!

We'll have news and pictures from Opry Cruise 2004 when we return to this space next week. But for now, has anybody seen my suntan lotion??

When my female fiddle player married Blake Shelton's male fiddle player, Blake said to me, "I guess this makes us artists-in-law."

February 2, 2004

Who was it that first said, "The best laid plans of mice and men oft' times go astray?" Whoever it was must have been reading my mail! As you know if you visit our web site often, last week was the 7th Annual Grand Ole Opry Cruise to the Caribbean. I had been looking forward to this cruise for a long time, because in addition to the fun and sun, the making of music and memories with our fans and friends, I was taking my daughter, Terri, and her husband, Grant, not only on their first cruise, but on their first vacation in almost five years. It was hard to tell who was more excited, dad or daughter.

All went perfect until Wednesday night when Grant became extremely ill during dinner. When his condition didn't improve after his resting for awhile, we took him to the ship's infirmary where they ran some tests and speculated that he might have suffered a heart attack. The ship's captain was told of the situation, and guided the ship into Grand Cayman an hour earlier than scheduled Thursday morning. Grant was rushed by ambulance to the main hospital on the island where more tests were run. I could not in good conscience leave Terri in a strange place so far away from home to handle such a tenuous situation by herself, so I excused myself from the cruise and stayed with her and Grant.

Long story short, the doctors ruled out a heart attack, but think now the problem may be neurological. We're all safely back in Nashville where Grant will be evaluated this week by his own doctors. I ask that you please keep him in your prayers.

To the many fans and friends aboard the ship, I apologize for having to leave the way I did, but I feel sure you understand. To the folks on Grand Cayman, especially the doctors and nurses at the Cayman Islands Government Hospital, your compassion and caring won't soon be forgotten. To Brad Paisley, Trace Adkins, Jim Ed Brown, Jeannie Seely, Eddie Stubbs, the Po' Folks Band, tour coordinator Joe DeFranco and his staff from Corporate Travel, along with Opry manager Pete Fisher, I know the shows went on without a hitch because you are all consummate professionals. (And Brad, we'll still finish that song together. It will just be on dry land somewhere instead of on the open seas!)

I did get to attend the all-day autograph party on Monday, host our fan club luncheon on Tuesday, and perform my full concert on Tuesday evening. I hope you'll check our News page for pictures from those events which we hope to have posted soon. As I once wrote and sang, "It was fun while it lasted...but it just didn't last long enough!"

However, if the Good Lord's willing and the creeks don't rise, as Hank used to say, I'll see you folks Friday night on the Opry and Saturday night in Ottawa, Kansas!

My thanks and best to you all.

Crusin' on the high seas with Trace Adkins, and Terri Clark

A wise country music singer once said about the recording process: "You never finish making a record. You just give up."

February 10, 2004

It's hard to believe on this chilly winter morning that it's time to begin thinking about our eighth annual City Lights Festival coming up in June, but I'm in Commerce, Georgia today holding a press conference, announcing the talent for this year's event, and I wanted to pass the information along to you as well.

This year's Festival, a two-day charity event from which the proceeds will go toward the building of a Performing Arts Center in the local community, will be held June 17th and 18th, and will feature live performances by two country music giants: Mel Tillis and Darryl Worley! Mel, of course, is a former CMA Entertainer of the Year, a singing and comedic talent beyond compare, and he'll be bringing with him his entire award winning band, The Statesiders. Darryl is one of country music's brightest young stars, having scored with such recent hits as "A Good Day To Run", "I Miss My Friend", and the thought-provoking patriotic anthem, "Have You Forgotten." Mel and Darryl will headline the big outdoor concert on Friday night June 18th at Tiger Stadium.

The Festival gets underway on Thursday, however, with our annual celebrity golf tournament at Sandy Creek golf course followed by the always popular "Dinner With The Stars" Thursday night at the local Civic Center. These dinners are informal events that feature the stars in an informal setting of good food, acoustical music, and lots of laughter. This year's dinner guests will include longtime Grand Ole Opry favorite, Jack Greene, his talented 17-year old singing partner, Candi Carpenter, the always gracious and popular Opry star, Jan Howard, and Hollywood comedian Dick Hardwick.

Of course, ole Whisperin' Bill will be around for all the festivities, and we've even added an event for our fan club members this year. We are planning a Members Only luncheon on Friday at a time and place to be announced later.

For those of you who have never been to one of our Festivals, it's a wonderful event held in a friendly community that traditionally welcomes our visitors with big smiles and lots of warm Southern hospitality. The festivities even continue on into Saturday with a variety of local events and activities.

We'll have more details as the time approaches and, who knows, maybe even an extra surprise or two to go along with this already fantastic lineup. Commerce is easy to reach, located just off I-85 about an hour's drive northeast of Atlanta. You can get ticket information by calling our toll-free hotline at 1-800-XXX-XXXX. Y'all come!!

* * * * * * * * * * * * * *

Many of you have written to ask about my son-in-law, Grant, who was taken off the Opry Cruise a few days ago and rushed to the hospital on Grand Cayman Island.

He's feeling much better, and the doctors are in the process of trying to determine just what caused his illness. The way I understand it, they are attempting to find out what it's NOT in hopes of eliminating everything except what it IS. He's continuing to have all kinds of tests run, and as soon as we know something definite I'll surely pass it along. Meantime, thanks so much for all your e-mails and your prayers. They are most appreciated.

Mel Tillis

February 23, 2004

Years ago, I used to think I wanted to be a newspaper columnist, and in particular, a sportswriter. I would read my favorite writers every day and think how wonderful it must be to watch ball games and then write about them for a living.

However, since I started hosting these little web site visits with you each week, I have come to realize something I never thought about back then: Before you can write something, you have to have an IDEA!!

It's been almost two weeks since I posted my last message to you here, and I have absolutely no idea at all what I'm going to write about today. Maybe it's a good thing that I became a songwriter instead of a columnist: Songwriters don't have to be creative on demand.

Come to think of it, songwriting has a lot of advantages. When I do write, I don't have to punch a time clock or sit behind a desk inside an office. I can write without a deadline and without pressure...other than the wolf clawing at the door. And I never have to write in a coat and tie. I wrote a song with a friend of mine on a warm day recently and he was wearing a faded t-shirt, khaki shorts, and flip-flops. Me? I dressed up fancy. I wore sweat pants, an old football jersey, a ball cap and tennis shoes. He laughed and said, "One of the best things about songwriting is the uniforms we get to wear."

Of course, you DO have to have an idea for a song, too, but that's what the co-writer is for. When I don't have an idea, my co-writer is supposed to have one. If he or she doesn't have one, then I usually come up with the best idea of all: Let's forget about writing and go to lunch! What a life!

xxxxxxxxxx

Two quick things: One, the tickets for the City Lights Festival in Commerce, Georgia, go on sale March 15th. That toll-free number again is 1-800-XXX-XXXX and the Festival dates are June 17th through the 19th. And, two, thanks for all your continued inquiries about my son-in-law who fell ill on the Opry cruise. We expect to hear more from his doctors in a few days, and I'll keep you posted.

Now if I can just come up with an idea of something to write about.....

March 3, 2004

My sister, Mary, was cleaning out a closet at our parents' house last week when she came across a beautiful cashmere sweater that Mama had given Daddy on a special occasion several years ago. The sweater was still in its original gift box. The card Mama had carefully selected was lying on top of the sweater. The tags had never been removed. There were several small holes in the sweater, obviously the handiwork of some mischievous and hungry little moths.

Knowing Mama, she had pinched her pennies for quite some time to afford such a luxurious gift. Knowing Daddy, he appreciated it greatly, but was saving it to wear on "just the right occasion"...an occasion that never came and now will never come.

This time last year, Mary learned that she had cancer. She and I have

discussed many times the unique vantage point from which she now views life. "I am living every moment like it might be the last," she says. "It's all so short and fragile, and we worry about all the wrong things."

To me, it's so sad that Daddy never wore his sweater. He didn't need to wait for a special occasion. LIFE is a special occasion. He didn't need to wait for the perfect time. ANYTIME would have been the perfect time.

Remember the old country song, "Put It Off Until Tomorrow?" I always liked that song, but the logic is faulty. If we keep putting things off until tomorrow, someday the tomorrows will run out. My sister is right. Life needs to be lived and celebrated every single day. Otherwise we run the risk of the moths eating holes in our dreams.

Photo: Bill's sister - Mary Hoyt

March 15, 2004

I have never been very good at keeping secrets.

So when Brad Paisley told me a couple of weeks ago not to mention ANYTHING about his next single record release to ANYBODY, I got nervous. Could I do it?? I seriously had my doubts.

But I am here today to report that I passed the test with flying colors, and this very moment is the first time I've told a soul 100%-for-sure that the song I co-wrote with Jon Randall called "Whiskey Lullaby" is going to be Brad's next single!

OK, I may have "hinted" at it when I sang the song on stage in Florida couple of weeks ago. My band may have "guessed" at it when I called a special rehearsal to work up our own arrangement on the song. But did I actually TELL anybody? Not that I recall.

This is exciting to me for several reasons. First, Brad is one of my closest buddies among the young country artists, and I love him like a little brother. He's written or co-written most of his own singles up to now, and I'm honored and thrilled that he's chosen a song that I helped create to further his career. Second, this is a COUNTRY song made even more country and more beautiful by the addition of Alison Krauss' angelic voice. I can actually envision Brad and Alison being nominated for Vocal Event of the Year for this sterling performance. And third, the decision to release it as a single was not made until Brad and Alison performed the song live for several hundred radio programmers at the recent Country Radio Seminar. Only when it received a standing ovation from one of the toughest audiences in the world was the single release a done deal.

He didn't say so, but I think Brad was afraid that talking about it up-front might jinx the whole thing. Now the official "Impact Date" of the record is March 29th. That's the date the label will be officially asking your local radio stations to play it, and I hope you'll be listening for it.

"People tell me that the song reminds them of 'He Stopped Loving Her Today'," Brad quips, "but only one person dies in that song. Two people die in ours."

But, please, don't tell anybody. That'll spoil the ending. And you know how Brad is about wanting to keep things secret!

March 23, 2004

We've all heard it: "In the Spring a young man's fancy turns to love."
Well, it's Spring again, and once again my fancy has turned not to love
but to that other great American pastime, the game of baseball. I guess
that's proof enough that I am no longer considered young!
Truth be known, my fancy used to turn to baseball in the Spring even
when I was a teenager. I'm not saying I never fell in love, because I did.
Every fifteen minutes or so there for awhile. But love is fleeting. Baseball
is forever.
I probably played in my first game of baseball about the time I started
kindergarten. My dad took me to see my first professional game when I
was eight, and I took my mom to see her first game when she was thir-
ty-five. I was hooked early on, but not until I attended my first major
league Spring training game in the late sixties did I discover baseball's
most joyous charm.
I guess it's partly because it's Spring and partly because it's the end of
Winter. It's partly the crack of the bat and partly the warmth of the sunshine. It's the cozy little ball parks, the rookie player making the circus
catch, the grizzled veteran struggling to extract one more base hit from
his well-worn Louisville Slugger, and these Winter-weary bones standing
up for one more national anthem and one more seventh inning stretch.
I'll be in Florida watching the Braves, the Tigers, the Indians, the Mets,
and whatever other assorted teams my buddies and I can squeeze into
the schedule for the next few days. It's my favorite time of year, because
in Spring training every team is a pennant winner, and every last place
team rises from worst to first. Remember the '91 Twins? Who says it
couldn't be the Tigers in 2004?
Hope springs eternal in the heart of every baseball fan come March. It's
the one time of year when the true fan forgets about the ridiculous
salaries, the ludicrous off season re-distribution of players (most of them
from elsewhere to the New York Yankees), the "Wait'll next year" cry of
the Chicago Cubs and the Boston Red Sox, and the annual swoon of the
Texas Rangers.
Right now the grass is mowed, the chalk lines sparkle in the daylight, the
uniforms are crisp and clean, and the umpire yells the two most beautiful
words in all of sports: "Play Ball."

Excuse me while I put my guitar back in its case for a few days. There's a ballpark hot dog and a cold beer calling my name from somewhere near Orlando.

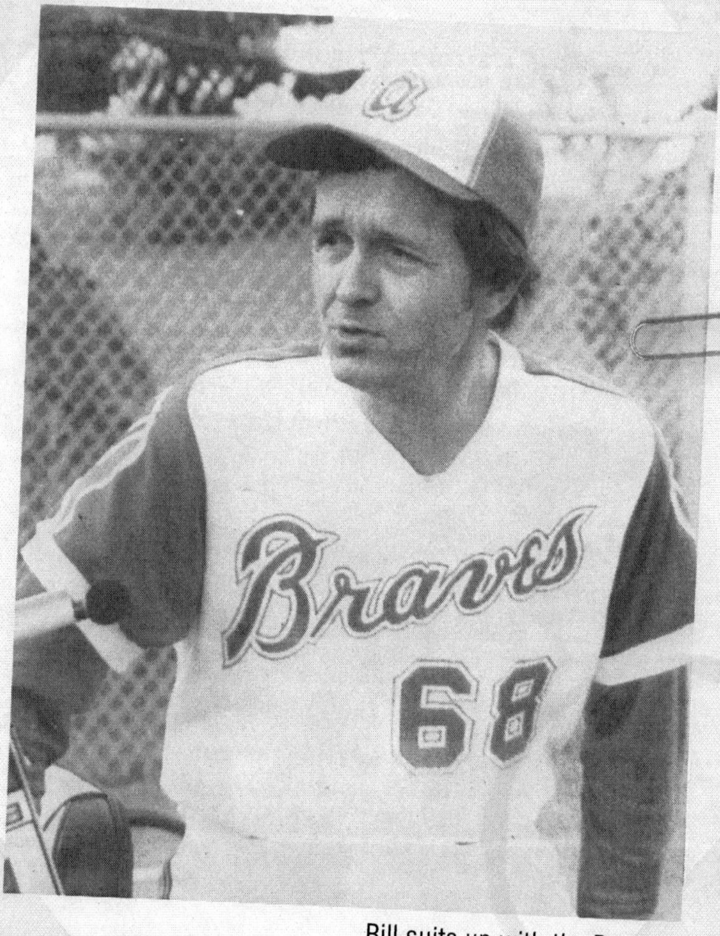

Bill suits up with the Braves.

March 30, 2004

I'll never cease to be amazed at how the simple ringing of a telephone can so often completely change a life.

I'll always remember the morning I was getting dressed to fly to Chicago to throw out the first pitch at a Cubs game and my secretary phoned to tell me to turn on my television. It was September 11, 2001.

Nor will I forget the piercing tone of my cell phone ringing in the little hotel room in Canada on an otherwise peaceful Sunday afternoon last fall, bringing me the emotional voice of my sister from thousands of miles away telling me my dad had passed away at noon.

Not all phone calls come bearing negative news, however, thank goodness. I got a happy call last week, one that I almost didn't answer. But I sure am glad I did.

I was ordering some food to go from a drive-in restaurant when the shrill ringing of my cell phone startled both me and the waitress who stood at my car window patiently taking my order. "It always rings at the wrong time," I opined, tempted to just let my voice mail answer. "Go ahead and get it," the young girl said. "I'm in no hurry." So I reached for the phone and mumbled, "Hello."

It was my daughter, Jenni, on the line calling from her home in south Georgia. We exchanged pleasantries, I told her what I was doing (she had called me while she was going through the drive-thru at McDonalds just a few days earlier!), and she said she wouldn't keep me but a minute. Then she asked those four words that a parent either loves or dreads to hear: "Are you sitting down?"

I assured her that I always try to sit down when I drive the car. She laughed and proceeded to tell me that she and her husband, Chuck, were expecting again! This would be their fourth child...due in October. I'm sure I shrieked (or screamed as loud as ole Whisperin' Bill is capable of screaming) and blurted out a series of rapid-fire questions. Then I asked, as any potential grandpa-to-be would ask, "What do the kids think about it?" Jenni laughed again.

"Well, Rachel (the oldest) said, 'Great, I'll have another kid to boss around!' Caroline (the nurturer) patted my belly, leaned in and said softly, 'How's my baby doing?' And Nick, (the three-year old) looked at his two sisters without cracking a smile said, "Let's get a boy!'"

I wrote in this space a few months ago that my son, Jamey, and his wife, Beth, are expecting their second child (a boy, by the way!) in August, so I am now going to be a new grandpa twice before this calendar year is over.

Sometimes the ringing of a telephone can bring incredible joy.

Lto R: Chuck, Nick, Jenni, Caroline, Rachel

April 6, 2004

Celebrity can sometimes be a funny thing, and I'm not just talking about Brad Paisley's recording of a song by that title.

Our Nashville newspaper recently asked its readers to submit stories of any personal encounters they may have had with celebrities outside of the celebrity's natural environment. Somebody told of meeting Alan Jackson while shopping at Target. Another saw pro football star Eddie George buying Christmas presents at midnight. One lived next door to Oprah when she was a local newscaster here and said Oprah's dog "used to poop in my yard."

Overall, there were some funny and poignant moments shared, but I wonder if anyone has ever considered doing the same story in reverse. How about the same scenario from a celebrity's point of view?

Vince Gill, who admits to loving to write and perform music but who says he is uncomfortable with "the whole celebrity thing," told a funny story recently on my radio show. He said he was walking through a mall when two ladies passed by and he overheard their conversation.

"Why, that man looks like Vince Gill!" one of the ladies exclaimed.

The other took a drag off her cigarette and replied sarcastically , "He wishes!"

I recently noticed a lady staring at me across the departure lounge at an airport. I was beginning to feel a bit uncomfortable when she rose from her chair and walked over to where I was sitting. "Aren't you a country music singer?" she asked.

"Yes, m'am," I said with a smile.

"Please forgive me, but I know your name," she continued. "I just can't think of it right now."

"Bill Anderson," I replied.

"No," she said, scratching her head, "that's not it."

I told her I was sorry, but that was the best I could do.

Like I say, celebrity can sometimes be a funny thing.

April 13, 2004

I sometimes think every person on earth must fancy himself or herself a songwriter.

I called an out-of-town florist today to order some flowers for the funeral of my former next door neighbor, and after I placed the order and told the lady what I wanted written on the card she said, "While I've got you on the phone, may I ask you a question?"

Years of experience told me what was coming. "I am a songwriter," she began, "and I don't know how to go about getting somebody to listen to my songs."

I probably get two dozen e-mails a week asking me the same question. People constantly stop me on the street, in shopping malls, at service stations, in convenience stores and, of course, at concerts and want to know what they have to do in order to get someone to listen to what they have written.

The temptation is to sometimes say, "Hey, I have enough trouble getting my own songs heard," but I try to recall those days years ago when I sat at my little manual typewriter all hours of the night writing letters to music publishers asking…no, begging…them to listen to some songs written by this eighteen year old college student.

Fortunately, today, there is an easier way. The Nashville Songwriters Association, International, has a division dedicated to helping aspiring writers, and I highly recommended to the lady in the flower shop (and to anyone else interested in songwriting) that she contact them. Their web site is

"http://www.nashvillesongwriters.com"

A small music publisher in Texas was the only one to reply to my letter back in 1956 saying I could send him my songs. Within a year I had sent him a song called "City Lights."

We later laughed over how prophetic he had been in his original letter. He said, "Sure, send me your songs. You never know where the next hit is coming from."

April 21, 2004

Hi....

And welcome to our web site.
If you're a first-time visitor, we're glad you stopped by and hope you can stay long enough to check out the many various features our site offers. For our regulars, it's always good to have you return.
Every couple of weeks or so, I try to post a personal message in this space, and I've received many favorable comments from those of you who come by to read my ramblings. As you know if you've ever written to me, I try awfully hard to respond to all my mail. Here lately, however, we've been having all kinds of problems with viruses and various other assorted gremlins getting inside our computers, and my mail has really become backed up. I can receive what you are sending to me, but I cannot seem to make the ole machine respond and send my letters back to you.
So, please don't think I am ignoring you. Even as I type this message, our people are working to get to the source of the problem. We'll solve it one way or the other, but we may end up having to change our mailing address in order to do so. Meantime, we'll keep the Tour page up-to-date and try to keep you informed on the News page. Our new gospel album will be available June 1st, and our Music and Merchandise pages will soon have samples for you to listen to and details on how to order your own personally autographed copy.
I'm sorry for the inconvenience. Thanks for bearing with us while we try to get things sorted out.

April 23, 2004

I am almost six-feet two-inches tall and he stands only four-feet eleven, but there is no one in this world that I look up to more than I look up to Little Jimmy Dickens.
He admits to being 83-years young and has recently undergone two serious surgeries. And yet at a time in his life when most people would

31

be rocking gently on their front porches caressing their memories, he is on airplanes and in busses and on stages all across America entertaining audiences like a twenty-year old.

He and I worked together last weekend in Kansas. When I got to the venue, he had already been there for more than an hour. On the first show at six o'clock, he sang his hits, told his jokes, and left the stage to a standing ovation. When the show was over, he stood behind a table down front and signed every autograph he was asked to sign. And then, just prior to the second show at nine-thirty, he informed us that he was ADDING a song to his upcoming performance. "I didn't get to do 'Raggedy Ann' on the first show because of the time limits," he said, "and I know lots of folks come to see that little doll. I'll put her into the second show." And he did.

Then he stood down front again until well past midnight meeting folks, posing for pictures, and autographing their souvenirs. He was in the hotel lobby long before I was the next morning cracking jokes, smiling, and signing more autographs. At the airport, more of the same. One lady told him that she had at one time lived next door to his mother in Arkansas. Jim's mom was from West Virginia and "never went outside the county," but when this lady insisted that his mom once lived in Arkansas, he simply smiled and said, "Well, maybe you know something about her that I don't know." I know lots of entertainers…including the one in my mirror…who would have never been that patient.

He has no idea I am writing this, and I have no special reason for it other than to share with you part of the thrill of being this man's friend. He should be declared a National Treasure…because that's exactly what he is.

Little Jimmy Dickens

May 3, 2004

Hi...

And welcome to our web site. If you're a first-time visitor or one of our many regulars, I hope you'll always feel at home here.

Most of you probably know that I came to Nashville many years ago to be a songwriter, and while I've been very fortunate to have had a career that has touched many other areas of show business as well, songwriting was and is and probably always will be my first love.

People ask me all the time how many songs I've written, and I have no idea. They want to know if such-and-such an artist ever recorded one of my songs, and quite often I don't know that either. It has occurred to me recently that I should have a better handle on such things, and with that in mind, my longtime assistant, Kathy Gaddy, and I have gone to work compiling as complete a list as we can find of the songs I've had recorded over the years and the artists who have performed them. Famous singers and unknowns...on major labels and small...we've come up with a list, and it's now posted here on our Music page under Discography.

I know this list is not 100% accurate and up-to-date, but it's a start. And I'm asking for your help. If you know of any songs of mine that are not listed here...or any versions by artists other than the ones we have listed...would you let me know? If you're ever going through your record collection and see my name listed as the writer of a particular song and it's not on this list, please bring it to my attention. (Please send U.S. releases only, as I cannot begin to list all the foreign recordings in all the various languages.)

This will be a never-ending and constantly-ongoing project, I'm sure, but with your help maybe someday my grandchildren will have a better idea of what their PawPaw did with his time and the talent with which God so richly blessed him.

Thanks so much.

Roger Miller, who was the closest thing to a genius that I have ever known, once declared: "The human mind in a wonderful thing. It starts working from before you're born and doesn't stop until you sit down and try to write a song."

May 17, 2004

My daddy used to tell me, "Son, there are two things you should never watch being made: laws and sausage."
Daddy might not be real proud of me today.
I just returned from a trip to Washington, D.C., where I visited with my longtime friend, Senator Zell Miller from Georgia, followed by a train trip down to Virginia where I hung out for a couple of days with the sausage king himself, Jimmy Dean. I did see laws being made (or at least votes being taken on the floor of the U.S. Senate), but Jimmy did not grind any sausage while I was there. However, let it be known that anytime he and I are together in the same room, there's enough ham present to end world hunger!
I made myself a promise about a year ago. I've worked awfully hard most of my life, and I've not devoted a whole lot of time to doing many things just for the pure personal enjoyment of it. My promise has been to correct that by occasionally slipping off onto some of life's side roads and spending a little time "smelling the roses."
Jimmy and his wonderful wife, Donna, have a gorgeous estate where I literally smelled roses and magnolias and honeysuckle and laughed until my sides hurt. At the Capitol, Senator Miller introduced me to Senator Orin Hatch from Utah who, I discovered, is a songwriter walking around in a Senator's body. We ate lunch in the Senate Dining Room, then retreated to Senator Hatch's office where we spent nearly an hour listening to some of his compositions and vowing to get together someday and co-write. I met Senator Jim Bunning from Kentucky, a former major league pitching hero of mine, who debunked the myth that Mickey Mantle once hit a home run off him one-handed.
I watched from the front row of the Senate gallery as two pieces of legislation were voted on, and I was no more than a few feet away from Senator Ted Kennedy, Senator John Edwards, Senator John McCain, and others. I heard Senator Hillary Clinton deliver an impassioned speech on funding for special education, and was seated next to Senator Miller when he was called to leave the chamber in order to go look at some horrible pictures from Iraq. Regardless of one's political persuasion, this was pretty heady stuff.

I went off and left my desk piled high with paperwork, but you know what? It was still there when I got home. I have tons of unanswered e-mail on my computer, and nobody volunteered to answer it for me while I was gone, but I'll figure out a way to get to most of it someday soon. Meantime, the roses sure smelled good, and I thoroughly enjoyed the detour.

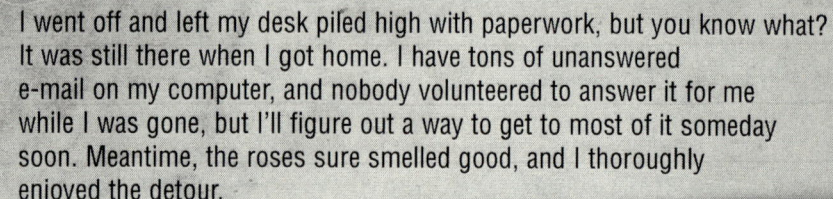

Little Jimmy Dickens,
Jimmy Dean and Bill

Jimmy Dean

Catch of the Day

May 27, 2004

May I have your attention please?

As you probably know, the Grand Ole Opry hosts a country music cruise to the Caribbean every year. The next one is set for January 22nd to January 29th, 2005.

Confirmed entertainers already include Little Jimmy Dickens, Trace Adkins, myself, and the Po' Folks Band . We have been assured that even more stars will be added.

These week-long Opry cruises are the highlight of any country music fan's year…as each winter we cruise aboard Carnival Cruise Lines to some of the most incredible ports of call imaginable. Just imagine your-self in January lying on a beach, sunning by a pool, shopping and dining and sightseeing, and having some of your favorite country entertainers right alongside. Ask anyone who has ever been on a Grand Ole Opry cruise….there's nothing quite like it.

So why am I telling you something you probably already know? Because this coming January, the Bill Anderson Fan Club is going to be giving away a Grand Ole Opry Cruise for two ABSOLUTELY FREE to one of our lucky fan club members!!

Do I have your attention now??

Every single member of our fan club that is in good standing as of October 15, 2004, will be eligible for this sweepstakes drawing. And everything will be furnished to the winner: Round-trip air fare and ground transportation from Nashville to our sailing destination of Port Canaveral, Florida, all port taxes, and all cruising amenities such as a cabin for two, all meals, all Grand Ole Opry shows (and there's one every day!), cocktail parties and autograph sessions with the stars…and it will all be ABSOLUTELY FREE!

If you're already one of our fan club members, thank you. Just make sure your dues are paid up through October 15th and your name will automatically go into the drawing. If you are not a member but would like to join and become eligible for the vacation of a lifetime, just click onto the Fan Club section of our web site, fill out the application blank, become a fan club member, and you'll have as good a chance as anyone of winning and going on the cruise with us.

The drawing will be held in Nashville on my birthday, November 1st. We will draw one winner and both a first and second alternate winner in case somebody wins but is unable to go. The prize is non-transferable, and you will be responsible for your own gratuities and incidental expenses. Fan Club memberships are very reasonably priced, and you'll get all the benefits of the club when you join...our Whisper-Journals three times a year, a free autographed color photo, tour updates, and other activities too numerous to mention. PLUS this one-time opportunity to cruise with the stars absolutely free.

Check it out. Who knows, we might just be cruising the high seas together come January. I'm already excited. How about you?

Jimmy Dean says that he once played at a fair so far back in the woods that the fair manager was a bear.

Photo Taken on Board Opry Crusie
Jean Brown, Fan Club President

June 8, 2004

Hi Gang:

A few weeks ago I wrote in this space about our efforts to revise and update the list of songs I have written that have been recorded either by me or by other various artists. I asked for your help in helping me make this list as complete as possible.

Several of you wrote and told me of songs that had been left off the list and artists who had recorded certain songs that I had failed to mention. I really appreciated your overwhelming response, but I have a confession to make: Quite a few of your e-mails got accidentally deleted before I could make the additions and changes to the list. Therefore, not all the changes have been made.

If you go to our Music section and click onto Discography and then onto the list of songs and you see a song that you know should be there and it isn't, could I ask you to please send it to me again? Several of you sent song titles that I recorded but didn't write (the song "Melinda," for example, was submitted several times, but Jimmy Gateley wrote that one, not me), but I'm only looking for my own compositions. Sorry to have to ask you to do this, but please know that it's more than appreciated.

We're gearing up for Fan Fair week (sorry, but it will always be Fan Fair to me) and it'll be a busy time. I have been to every Fan Fair except one since 1974, and I always look forward to meeting lots of old friends and making new ones. Our booth is #726, and I hope lots of our web-site buddies will stop by. We'll also be appearing on all the Opry shows this week as well as the Superstar Spectacular on Thursday night. If you can't be here for the festivities, I hope you'll tune us in on WSM, on the internet, or on Sirius Satellite Radio.

Thanks and my best as always,

June 15, 2004

Hi Gang:

Well, I'll be leaving Nashville tomorrow headed south to my adopted hometown of Commerce, Georgia, for our 8th Annual City Lights Festival, and I hope to see lots of our web site buddies while I'm there.

I'm sure you know by now that Mel Tillis and Darryl Worley will be headlining our big outdoor show on Friday night June 18th (please say a little prayer for good weather!), along with Jack Greene, Jan Howard, Con Hunley, the Jordans, myself and the Po' Folks Band. For those of you in the southeast, Commerce is about halfway between Atlanta and Greenville, S.C. right off of Interstate 85, and at our Festivals we always have room for one more!

It was great seeing so many of you during Fan Fair....er, the CMA Music Festival. I performed on six different shows last week and spent a total of seven hours signing autographs and meeting folks in my fan club booth, so I know I crossed paths with a whole lot of you. (You can check out pictures from our fan club dinner under the News section while you're on the web site.) I hope y'all enjoyed Nashville as much as we enjoyed having you in our city. Come back and see us again soon.

Meanwhile, I hope to see lots more good country fans in Commerce this coming weekend. Travel safe...and be sure to come up and say Howdy!

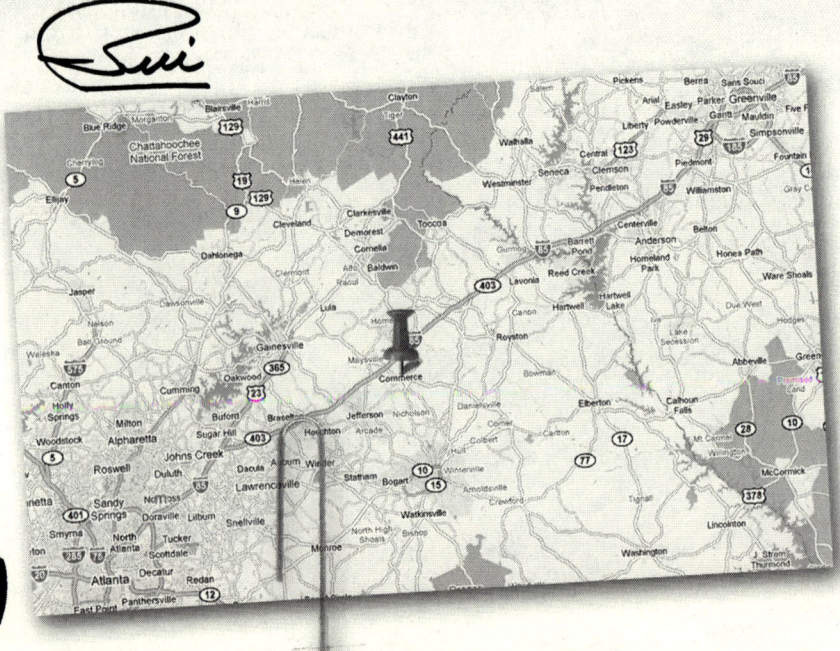

June 20, 2004

Hi Gang:

Just a quick note to thank the thousands of you who came from more than 20 states to take part in our 8th annual City Lights Festival this past weekend in my "adopted" hometown of Commerce, Georgia.

We had typical hot and humid Georgia weather, but the rain only teased us and passed on by. I met many of our web site buddies, and appreciated the chance to greet you face to face, many for the very first time.

I cannot thank my fellow entertainers enough: Mel Tillis and his great band, The Statesiders; the super-talented and always-gracious Darryl Worley and all his folks; Jack Greene and 17-year old future star, Candi Carpenter, my longtime buddy Jan Howard, Con Hunley, Les Singer and the Po' Folks Band, and the man who kept us laughing far into the night on Thursday, Dick Hardwick. You are each so professional and so giving of your time and your talents. "Thank you" seems such a small thing to say for such large contributions on your parts.

All our workers and volunteers deserve another special pat-on-the-back again this year, and at the risk of overlooking some, I'll even name a few: Gerald Jordan, Rob Jordan, LaVerne Bennett, Anthony Bennett, Eldon Collins, Pat Bell, Verlon Reese, Betty Hofer, Jim Purcell, and others too numerous to mention. Trust me, we couldn't do it without you.

To the folks who helped publicize the event, those who cooked and served the food and cleaned up afterward, those who parked the cars, took up the tickets....well, you get the idea. Most of all, thanks to those of you who came...and my regrets to any who might have missed the Friday concert because you were stuck in the terrible traffic tragedies on Interstate-85. Our deepest sympathies to the friends and families of those involved in the accidents.

I hope we can do it again next year...and I hope everyone who is reading this can be in Commerce with us. There's nothing quite like it, believe me.

July 2, 2004

Hi Folks:

Those of you who visit this space on a regular basis have noticed, no doubt, that I've been rather quiet for the past few days.

That's because following all the work that goes into Fan Fair and into our annual City Lights Festivals down in Georgia, I just don't have much energy left over for writing letters…or very much of anything else. (By the way, we've got lots of new pictures up in our News section from both these events in case you haven't seen them!)

That's also why I try to mark a few days off after these back-to-back gatherings to simply take a deep breath and relax. I pointed the nose of my car in a southward direction last Sunday and didn't stop until I ran out of land at the edge of the Gulf of Mexico. I've been enjoying a little time "with myself" which, as my daughter, Terri, points out is vastly different from time "by myself." I've recharged my batteries a bit, and as soon as the fireworks have finished lighting the southern skies on the 4th of July, I'll be headed back toward Music City and another hectic schedule.

I hope each of you has a wonderful holiday weekend. May we all continue to count our blessings as we commemorate and celebrate the founding of our great country. Be careful if you're traveling, and don't forget to toss those firecrackers as soon as you light them! Thanks for stopping by. I'll see you back here soon.

July 6, 2004

Do you like music videos?

Me too.

Me neither.

Nearly everyone I talk to on this subject seems to feel the same way. Yes, I like them. No, I don't. Truthfully, I think the answer lies somewhere in between for most of us. We like videos on some songs and we don't necessarily care for them…or feel as though we need them…on others. When Brad Paisley first recorded the song I co-wrote with Jon Randall, "Whiskey Lullaby," he said there would not be a video made on it. The song, he felt, painted such a vivid picture by itself that to make a video might infringe on each listener's own interpretation of the lyric. Kenny Chesney had said essentially the same thing about another song I had a hand in writing, "A Lot Of Things Different."

Kenny never did shoot a video to accompany his recording, but Brad and Alison Krauss have recanted and filmed a mini-movie depicting actor/director Ricky Schroeder's interpretation of "Whiskey Lullaby." And after seeing it, I'm really glad they did.

True, it's only one person's vision of the song, but what a powerful vision it is. I especially like the scene toward the end when the little girl looks back and sees the "ghosts" of the two people who supposedly drank themselves to death dancing together beneath the willow. I cried real tears the first time I saw it.

"Whiskey Lullaby" is a dark song written about a dark and touchy subject. Frankly, I was a bit afraid of how a video treatment might turn out. I'm happy to report that the video doesn't justify or glorify drinking, and it portrays the effects of drinking painfully, vividly, and honestly. It makes a highly emotional and effective point without condescending or preaching. I hope you'll like it when you see it, and I commend and thank everyone involved in the production for a job well done.

July 16, 2004

Hi:

And welcome to our web site, especially to our first-time visitors. We're glad you stopped by.

I got a phone call last night from my former singing partner and long-time Opry star, Jan Howard, that I haven't been able to get off my mind. I don't know how many of you know it, but Jan suffered a bad fire at her home back in May, and she's been living in a hotel for over three months. If all goes as planned, she'll finally get back into her own place late next week.

Even though I knew about the fire, caused by a faulty lamp in her office, I didn't realize until we were talking that Jan lost virtually all the memorabilia she had collected from her many years in country music. From the tone of her voice, I detected that this loss hurt her more than losing all the other valuables that were destroyed combined.

I think we ought to do something about it. Knowing country music fans as I do, I'll bet lots of you have pictures of Jan that you've taken over the years…perhaps extra copies of some of her recordings…magazine and newspaper articles…that you wouldn't mind parting with. Anything that might in some way relate to her career.

Why don't you see what you can find and let's start a little campaign to try and replace some of the things Jan lost and, at the same time, show her how much we love her and respect all that she has meant to country music all these years? If you've got anything you think Jan would like to have, send it to me at P.O. Box 888, Hermitage, TN. 37076, and I'll start putting together a Memory Book for her.

She has no idea I'm doing this…and I'm probably opening a big can of worms…but she'd do it for me, and I want to do it for her. Spread the word to your friends and fellow country music fans. They are having a Jan Howard Day in her hometown of West Plains, Missouri, on the 25th of September, and I'll present the Memory Book to her on that day. Hopefully, lots of you can even be there.

Send anything that you think she might like to have, and let's help put a smile back on a special lady's face.

Many thanks.

43

July 21, 2004

Hi Gang:

And welcome to our web site.

If this is your first visit, I probably need to tell you that I use this space from time to time to keep in touch with our friends and fans on a variety of subjects. Recently, I spent some time here talking about the amazing new video on the song Jon Randall and I co-wrote for Brad Paisley and Alison Krauss called "Whiskey Lullaby."

Well, that's not the only video out these days on one of my co-authored songs. It's just the only serious one.

I wrote a fun song a couple of years ago with The Warren Brothers, Brent and Brad, those wild and crazy guys who helped judge the most recent "Nashville Star" competition. It's a song about a singer who is trying to break into the big time but is temporarily, at least, stuck in the small bars and honky-tonks of obscurity. The song is called "Sell A Lot Of Beer" and the Warrens have released it as their current single. And they've accompanied the release of the song with exactly the kind of video you'd expect from two guys who, as Roger Miller used to say, "march to the beat of their own plumber." It's as funny as "Whiskey Lullaby" is sad. You might want to be watching for it.

There's also a new recording of an old song of mine on the market that I'm awfully proud of and excited about. Con Hunley, one of the greatest song stylists of our time, has recorded "Still" in a way you've never heard it sung before. I've often said that anyone can trace a picture, but it takes a true artist to paint one. Give a listen to Con's version of "Still" and you'll realize what a truly great artist this man is. So far there's no video in the works, but as photogenic as Con is, there ought to be. Meantime, it's some awfully good music for the ears.

Stay tuned and thanks again for stopping by. Enjoy your visit and come back soon.

I became more than a little anxious as to how our show might sound the afternoon we pulled into a fair in West Virginia. I looked out the window of our bus and saw a van parked beside the stage with a sign on the side that read, "Smith's Heating & Sound Company."

44

July 31, 2004

If you have ever had any contact with me through my office at Bill Anderson Enterprises here in Nashville, you have probably had contact with my administrative assistant, Kathy Gaddy, as well.

Kathy has been the friendly voice on our telephone for years, the smiling lady behind the front desk, and the right arm that every person in this business needs…especially if you're left-handed like me!

Kathy's mom, Jeanne, was my secretary from the late sixties until 1987. She started bringing Kathy around the office when Kathy was barely in her teens. When she was about fifteen years old, Kathy started coming in after school and helping us mail out my new record releases to the radio stations. She became the hostess for my syndicated television show not long after that, welcoming our studio audiences to the tapings and helping them to relax and feel comfortable. When she learned to type, we put her to work helping answer our mail. Gradually she became a very vital and important member of our office family.

When Kathy's mom left our organization to return to her native Texas, it was only natural that Kathy become my full-time assistant. She has served in that capacity ever since and has done an incredible job.

So why am I telling you all this? Because Kathy is about to retire after working for me for only 35-years. (Makes you wonder whatever happened to loyalty, doesn't it?)

We are having a retirement party for Kathy on August 29th, and I thought many of her friends would like to know and perhaps drop her a note and wish her well in her upcoming life of leisure. You can contact her via e-mail at Kathy@billanderson.com or via snail mail at P.O. Box 888, Hermitage, TN. 37076.

While you're sending her notes of congratulations, though, you might want to send me a sympathy card. 'Cause I sure am going to miss her.

August 6, 2004

Hi Gang:

Well, as of 7:45 Central time this morning there is another William Anderson on the planet!

Do you think the planet is ready for that?

My son, Jamey, and his wife, Beth, are the proud parents of 7 lb. 15 oz. Gary William Anderson, named for both of his grandfathers. They plan to call him Gabe.

I am happy to report that everybody is doing well, and Gabe arrived with all his fingers and toes along with a full head of dark black hair. To tell the truth, he looks almost identical to the way Jamey looked when he was born.

We took Gabe's older brother, Blake, to the hospital this morning to see this baby brother he has been hearing so much about. When Gabe was safely in his crib (is that what you call them?) in the nursery, I lifted Blake (he's 21-months old) up to the window so he could see.

I said, "Blake, there's your baby brother," and Blake began to point and smile and say, "Baby, baby." It was only when I looked closer that I realized Blake was not looking and pointing at his brother. He was pointing to another baby in the next crib, a cute little girl with a shiny pink ribbon in her hair. I don't think he has seen his brother yet, but he and little Miss Pink Ribbon are becoming very good friends!

He's a true Anderson all right! I just wonder how he's going to react when he realizes the little girl won't be going home with him and his brother will!

46

September 1, 2004

Hi Folks….
And welcome to our web site.
The Po' Folks Band and I are about to leave Nashville for an almost three-week swing of concert dates through eastern Canada, and we're looking forward to seeing lots of our friends and fans along the way. For all the details, click onto the Tour section and follow us in our travels.Before taking off, however, I wanted to remind you about a couple of important things.
First, you've only got until October 15th to sign up or renew your dues in our Fan Club in order to be eligible for the FREE Grand Ole Opry cruise for two that the club is giving away on November 1st. This is the cruise that will sail to the eastern Caribbean in January, 2005, and feature entertainment by Terri Clark, Little Jimmy Dickens, Trace Adkins, and myself. Some lucky member of our fan club will be invited to go with us all expenses paid. Go to our Fan Club section for details on how to join with us.
Also, as you know if you've been following these little columns recently, we are attempting to gather as much memorabilia as we can for our fellow Opry star, Jan Howard, who lost virtually all of her career keep-sakes during a recent fire at her home. If you've got any spare pictures of Jan you might have taken over the years, any magazine or newspaper articles about her, or anything relating to her musical career that you think she might like to have to replace what she lost, please get them to me no later than September 24th. We will present a special Memory Box to her on Jan Howard Day in West Plains, Missouri, September 25th.
My mailing address is P.O. Box 888, Hermitage, TN. 37076.
Thanks so much and my best wishes to you all.

September 21, 2004

Hi Folks:

Just a short note to let you know we are safely home from our long Canadian tour and that we had a wonderful time.

To all our fans up that way, thanks so much for coming to see us and for making us feel so welcome. To Kitty Wells, Johnny Wright, Bobby Wright, Jean Shepard, and George Hamilton IV, you each redefined the word "professionalism" every single night. Thanks for allowing me to share the miles and the stages with you.

We were, of course, all saddened on Sunday morning when the news reached us of Skeeter Davis' passing. She was a dear friend and an inspiration to us all. She will be greatly missed.

Don't forget we will be paying tribute to our friend, Jan Howard, this coming Saturday (25th) in her hometown of West Plains, Missouri. Thanks to all who sent replacement items for Jan's memorabilia collection. I'll present them to her on stage at the concert. I hope lots of you can be there.

Til next time, take care and thanks for everything.

Skeeter Davis

September 27, 2004

Hi Folks:

As I was typing the date for this note to you, I was struck by the fact that this day would have been my Mom and Dad's 71st wedding anniversary. You never get over missing them, do you?

I'm sure by now most of you know that in addition to Skeeter Davis, our country music family lost another great person and great artist last week when Roy Drusky passed away. What you may not know is that Roy engineered the very first recording I ever made.

He was a disc jockey at Radio Station WEAS in Decatur, Georgia, in the mid to late fifties, and I cut my first record in those studios. It was called "Take Me" and was backed with "Empty Room" and released on TNT Records about a year prior to my recording of "City Lights." I used to tease Roy and tell him that his career survived in spite of his having engineered my first record and his having recorded my silly song, "Peel Me A 'Nanner!" Roy was a gentle soul, and he will be missed.

Ray Price needs our thoughts and prayers these days, too. He was at first thought to have suffered a heart attack last week, but was found to have blockage which has now been treated. It took two of us, me and Little Jimmy Dickens, to fill in for Ray at the fair in Cullman, Alabama, Friday night, and there was still a big void. Singers like Ray Price are truly few and far between.

Because of the added date to my schedule, I didn't get to complete the Memory Box I started for Jan Howard and to which many of you contributed, but her "Day" in her hometown of West Plains, Missouri, was a rousing success nonetheless. She was quite touched by your generosity, and I'll get the memorabilia to her shortly.

Have a good week, and thanks for everything,

Grandpa Jones said he once performed at a theater that was so small, "I took a bow and my dandruff landed in the lobby."

October 5, 2004

Hi Folks:

People ask me all the time in interviews what my hobbies are, what things I enjoy doing when I'm not out on tour or holed up somewhere trying to write a song.

My answer is always the same: I'm a sports junkie. And when you are a sport junkie, this time of year is as good as it gets.

The baseball playoffs are about to begin and the World Series is just around the corner. Both college and professional football are in full swing, and my alma mater has the #3 ranked college team in the nation. The weather is beginning to cool, the leaves will be changing colors soon, and I live for my first cup of hot coffee on a bright autumn day, the rocking chair on the screened porch off my bedroom, and the morning sports section.

I've never made a big secret of which teams I pull for. Most of you know I'm a huge Braves fan (after all, I grew up in Atlanta!), a Tennessee Titans fan (that's kinda tough right now), and a big fan of my college alma mater, the Georgia Bulldogs. I take a lot of kidding from fans around the country who are fans of their local teams, but part of the fun of being a sports junkie is having someone to argue with, compare statistics with, and to enjoy the experience with.

If my son, Jamey, and I can't watch or listen to a game together, we are constantly on the phone back and forth while the game is going on, either discussing the action or one of us informing the other as to what is taking place on the field.

If Les Singer, my longtime guitar player and band leader, and I aren't arguing sports on the bus, the other members of the band think one or both of us is sick.

If you're not a sports fan, I'm sure this bores you to tears. But if you are, then I have only one thing to say:

"It's October...Play Ball!"

October 11, 2004

Hi Folks:

And thanks for stopping by our web site.

I had quite an experience Sunday that I want to share with you. We were booked to play an afternoon concert in the town where I was born and lived for the first eight years of my life, Columbia, South Carolina. Ironically, my son, Jamey, who is an airline pilot, had a twenty-four hour layover in Columbia on Saturday. I hadn't been to Columbia in almost twenty-five years, and Jamey and I had never been there together.

So, I drove into town early Sunday morning, picked him up at his hotel, and took him to see the house where my family used to live, the church we attended, the playground where I played as a child, and the building where I started school…which is now an apartment complex. I was amazed at how well I remembered the streets and how little trouble I had finding my way around. We saw the site of the old hospital where I was born, then enjoyed a delightful breakfast together virtually in the shadow of the old neighborhood. For Jamey, it was a part of my life that he had never been exposed to, and for me it was a very special time that I got to share with my son.

Shortly after noon, he left town flying a jet bound for Cincinnati, and I drove to the State Fairgrounds for our show. My own dad had taken me to my first fair on that very site many years ago. I had no sooner gotten out of my car than I came face-to-face with the neighbor lady who had taken me inside my very first radio station and let me watch my first live country music performers when I couldn't have been more than five or six years old.

Dean Martin once had a hit song called, "Memories Are Made Of This." That's what I was thinking Sunday as I relived some pretty special memories myself and made some great new ones.

Life doesn't get a whole lot better.

October 20, 2004

Hi Folks:

I have said many times over the years that I've never had the largest number of fans in country music, but I'll put the loyalty of the fans that I do have up against that of any other artist.

This loyalty, which I appreciate more than you'll ever know, has been demonstrated to me time and time again over the years and in more ways than you might ever imagine. But the past ten days have brought it to life one more time, and at the risk of embarrassing the participants, I want to share this with you.

Billie and Bob Hicklin, who have been married for 52-years, live in Kings Mountain, N.C. On Saturday night October 9th we performed in Gaffney, South Carolina, just south of their home. They bought tickets and drove to the show. Billie, who is our fan club representative for North Carolina, Virginia, and Kentucky, stayed around after the show and handed out fan club application blanks while I signed autographs, then she and her husband drove home for what was left of the night.

After going to church the next morning (Bob is a retired Baptist minister), they drove over a hundred miles south to Columbia, South Carolina, and when I walked on stage at three o'clock, I saw their smiling faces on the second row. Again, following the concert, Billie stood at my side recruiting new members for our fan club. As the sun set in the west, it was back to North Carolina for my special fans and friends.

Three days later, there the Hicklins were again right down front at our two o'clock show in Hiawassee, Georgia. Again, Billie stood by for another autograph session that lasted more than an hour, then when I took to the stage at eight o'clock that night, she and Bob were right there again. I teased and told her that by now she knew what I was going to sing before I even sang it!

The Hicklins didn't follow us to Kansas over the weekend (it wouldn't have surprised me if they had!), but in Raleigh, North Carolina, the following Tuesday they sat through two more shows and stood by my side through two more autograph sessions.

I can't add up the miles they drove, the money they spent for gasoline, the cost of their concert tickets, plus the wear and tear they put on their bodies, just to come see me and listen to our music. I get paid for doing this, and there were times during this stretch when I wondered what I was doing traveling so much, and yet here were fans of mine so loyal that they were traveling right along beside me, for nothing more than to simply show their friendship and their support.

Many of you have borne similar expenses and inconveniences on my behalf over the years and continue to do so. I just hope you know how much I appreciate it. You constantly remind of a line in a song I once recorded: "I, among men, am most richly blessed."

Billie Hicklin

October 28, 2004

Hi Gang:

And welcome to our web site.

There's a new slideshow from last week's Opry in the News section that features a picture of me and Sonny Osborne relaxing backstage. If you think the grin on Sonny's face was big then, you should see him this morning. My first e-mail of the day was a note from him in big capital letters: CAN YOU BELIEVE THE RED SOX ARE FINALLY WORLD CHAMPIONS! He is one happy camper today!

I want to remind any of our fan club members who may not have heard that our drawing for the free Grand Ole Opry cruise that was scheduled for November 1st has been moved to November 3rd. I've been asked to fill in once again for Ray Price on a show in Champaign, Illinois, on the 1st, so be listening to WSM at nine o'clock (CST) on Wednesday night the 3rd for our drawing. You can listen at AM650, via the internet, or on Sirius Satellite Radio Channel 137. I hope to make somebody real, real happy that night.

Thanks for all the birthday greetings you've been sending my way as well as the many congratulatory notes regarding the birth of my new grand-daughter, Greta Joy Robeson on October 23rd. Would you believe there was no photographer on duty at the small hospital in south Georgia to take her picture? I guess that's what happens when you're born at 3:30 a.m. on a Saturday! I haven't even had a glimpse of her yet, but from all I hear she's beautiful. I hope all is well in each of your worlds, and I thank you again for stopping by. Let's visit again soon.

Greta Joy Robeson

54

November 4, 2004

Hi Gang:

Well, for those of you who weren't by your radios last night, we held our big fan club drawing for a free Grand Ole Opry cruise over WSM, and it was "live radio" at its finest.

The winner turned out to be a twelve-year old girl from South Carolina named Emily Gantt. When we tried to call and give her the big news, though, we couldn't get her on the phone because her area code had been changed. When we finally did get through, she squealed with delight when she learned she had won...until her mom reminded her that the dates for the cruise overlapped with a school trip to Washington, D.C. for the Presidential Inauguration. I could tell on the phone she hated to turn down our trip, but I assured her that she (and her mom) definitely made the right choice.

So, we drew again. The winner this time was Shirley Smith from New Madison, Ohio. After we finally convinced her it wasn't a prank, I think she got pretty excited. However, we had some telephone difficulties with her too, and it resulted in our being disconnected. At that point I think Shirley thought for sure someone was playing a joke on her. Our fan club president, Jean Brown, spoke with her later, however, and convinced her that everything was on the level. Shirley plans to take her husband, and here's hoping they have the best time ever!

To those of you who joined the club or renewed your dues in order to be eligible for the drawing, many thanks. I hope you'll enjoy your membership with us and will stay around for many years (and hopefully many more drawings) to come. And to my buddy, Eddie Stubbs, thanks so much for allowing us to use your valuable air time to draw for the winner. You are a real pro and it shows in all that you say and do.

Before I go, let me thank you once again for all the birthday greetings, both e-mail and otherwise. My new assistant, Judy, was shocked at how many cards came to the office. I keep telling her I've got the greatest fans in the world. Keep this up and she'll start to believe me.

Smooth sailing to you all and thanks for everything,

November 10, 2004

Hi Gang:

They call it "Country Music's Biggest Night," and last night it certainly lived up to its billing.

I hope all of you were able to see the 38th Annual CMA Awards telecast live from Nashville. It was a lot of fun being there.

The song Jon Randall and I co-wrote, "Whiskey Lullaby," won in two of the four categories in which it was nominated, and all of us involved are so appreciative and grateful. It won an award for Brad Paisley and Alison Krauss as "Musical Event of the Year," and for "Video of the Year." We missed out on "Song of the Year" honors, the award which would have gone to us as the writers, but nobody here is complaining at all. Ours was a song that flew in the face of everything modern country music seems to be about these days, and it did so much better than any of us had dared to hope for. As I told Jon after the show, "We've had a heckuva ride!"

Plus, it's not tough when you lose to a song as great as the one written by two outstanding songwriters, Craig Wiseman and Tim Nichols, who wrote "Live Like You Were Dying." What an insightful and inspiring piece of work that song is, and I congratulate Craig, Tim, and Tim McGraw who recorded it.

The CMA Awards will look and feel a lot different next year because for the first time in history they'll be coming from New York instead of Nashville. It'll be interesting to see how that all works out. As the old saying goes, "Don't knock it 'til you've tried it."

My best to all, and again, thanks for being so good to our song.

Singer-songwriter Dusty Drake on having spent twelve years in Nashville looking for his big break in the music business: "I figured in two years I'd either be famous or gone. I'm neither."

56

November 18, 2004

Hi Gang:

One of my boyhood heroes was (and is) a sportswriter in Atlanta named Furman Bisher. When I was a teenager and attempting to be a bit of a sportswriter myself, I wanted to grow up to be him.

Every Thanksgiving he would write a column in the paper listing the things he was most thankful for that particular year. With apologies for borrowing his idea, I've made a little list of my own:

I'M THANKFUL....

For the sun that came up over the Tennessee hills this morning, and that I was able to get up out of bed, make coffee, and be gifted with another day as a small part of God's incredible creation.

I'm thankful that one is never considered "too old" to be a songwriter. I'm thankful for the gift of "Whiskey Lullaby", and the fact that it succeeded in spite of being so different from most of the songs on today's country radio.

I'm thankful for the lives and the legacies of those we've lost this year, including Skeeter Davis and Roy Drusky, who inspired me with their talents and honored me with their friendship. And I'm thankful that Kris Kristofferson and Jim Fogelsong received their just due by being inducted into the Country Music Hall of Fame.

I'm thankful that I got into the music business at a time when value was placed on each artist being a unique stylist and being different from others in the genre.

I'm thankful for the gift of laughter, and I'm glad I've had the good fortune of getting to know and laugh along with Roger Miller, Grandpa Jones, Minnie Pearl, Lewis Grizzard, Jimmy Dean, Jimmy Gateley, and Little Jimmy Dickens.

I'm thankful for the towns and cities along our concert trail that have sidewalks, hiking trails, and picturesque parks where I can go walking during my visits.

I'm thankful for having had the opportunity recently to re-visit the two houses of my childhood where I most remember growing up. But I sure thought the front yard of our house in South Carolina was bigger than it is!

57

As much as I miss my mom, I'm thankful she didn't have to live to experience the horror of 9/11....nor see our neat little white house on Conway Road now painted an outlandish shade of red with white trim. And yet I can't help but wonder what that witty and acerbic little lady would have said when she saw it!

I'm thankful my sister continues to stand toe-to-to with the Big C, fighting it has hard as anyone possibly could. I'm thankful she has learned to take each day as it comes...living with a grateful and determined attitude.

I'm thankful for the birth of two new grandchildren this year, and the wonderful love and joy I continue to receive from the four that were already here.

I'm thankful for three children, two sons-in-law, and a daughter-in-law who bless and brighten my life every day. I'm especially thankful for my son's unshakable faith in the face of all the uncertainties within the airline industry these days...an industry he loves and in which he is employed.

I'm thankful for our servicemen and women who, by no choice of their own, must spend Thanksgiving apart from their friends and families this year because they are somewhere helping protect the freedoms the rest of us too often take for granted.

I'm thankful for the little 85-year old lady who proudly told me, "I've listened to you all my life!"

And I'm thankful for each of you, my fans and my friends, who stopped by my web site today. May we each be renewed by the season and reminded of our many, many blessings...not just at Thanksgiving, but on every single day of the year.

Hope springs eternal in the heart of a songwriter. "My goal in life is to write a meaningful song that is good enough to record," a lady once told me. "I did get a little encouragement recently when one of my songs was stolen."

December 06, 2004

Hi Gang:

It's the holiday season and I know you don't have much time for reading, and I don't have a whole lot of time for writing. But I thought I'd share a couple of things with you that might just bring a smile to your face during this hectic season.

I met a lady at the Country Music Hall of Fame on Friday who told me that she wanted me to sing at her funeral. I told her that I appreciated the honor, but that I'm just too emotional a person to sing funeral-type music.

To which the lady responded, "I don't care. I still want you to sing at my funeral. And it doesn't have to be a sad song. If you want to, you can sing, 'I'm Gonna Have A Wild Weekend' !!"

I think maybe I'll pass on that!

Second, I want to verify a rumor going around. It's absolutely true. Based on the recent success of the new duo, "Big & Rich," me and Jimmy Dickens are forming a team to be known as "Little & Po!"

"We'll work concerts for half as much money as they do," Little Jim said, "and we'll even do a matinee!"

If there's anything more fun than the country music business, I have yet to find it.

Happy Holidays,

From the mail bag: "I can't see. I am 99% blind. And I don't like the way these young singers dress."

A musician's definition of a record producer: "A person who doesn't know what he wants and, by God, knows how to get it."

A banjo player told me this one: Banjo players spend half of their life tuning and the other half playing out of tune.

December 14, 2004

Hi Gang:

Not long after I moved to Nashville, I clipped an article out of the local newspaper and carried in my wallet until it finally disintegrated with age. It simply said:

"Find Something You Like Doing So Much You'd Do It For Nothing. Then Learn To Do It So Well That They'll Pay You, And You've Got It Made."

At that time in my life, I had already found my "something"....writing songs and entertaining people. Nobody was paying me for it quite yet, but I loved it so much I knew I'd do it for nothing if I had to. And I did do it for next-to-nothing for a long time!

In later years, I wanted to share this bit of wisdom with a group of high school students that I had been asked to address on their annual Career Day, so I had a few hundred cards printed and passed them out after my talk. I always wondered if the kids tossed them in the trash as soon as my back was turned.

I got my answer a few days ago when I happened to cross paths with one of those former students. He is now 26-years old, married, and has one child. As soon as he spotted me, he reached into his wallet and pulled out the worn, crumpled card I had given him at least ten years before and said, "I want to thank you for this. I've carried it ever since you gave it to me."

"And are you now doing something you love and getting paid for it?" I asked.

"I sure am," he smiled, "and the words on this card have had a lot to do with that."

Are you looking for something to give to a young person for Christmas? Print those few words out and slip them under the tree or into a stocking. You might just encourage someone to follow their passion in life no matter how foolish or futile it might seem at the time.

Is there a better gift you could give?

Happy Holidays,

December 22, 2004

MERRY CHRISTMAS, GANG, AND A VERY HAPPY NEW YEAR
TO EACH OF YOU!
SEE YOU BACK IN THIS SPACE IN '05!!

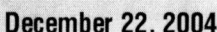

2005

January 3, 2005

Hi Gang:

And a Happy New Year to you all!

Back before the holidays, I spoke with Barbara Mandrell for my XM satellite radio Christmas special, and I asked her what she had been doing lately. "Not much," she replied, "I've retired."

The word "retired" had a strange ring to it, because in the history of professional country music, it's a word that hasn't often been used. When you think of names like Roy Acuff, Ernest Tubb, Red Foley, and Bill Monroe, for example, you don't think retirement. You think of happy road warriors who picked and grinned until there simply weren't any more auditoriums left to play and no more G-chords left to strum. Even the great Eddy Arnold waited until his 80th birthday to quit performing, and I heard a rumor the other day that he has recently been back in the recording studio singing again.

Carl Smith, Tom T. Hall, Sonny James, the Statlers, and Barbara are the exceptions I can think of. They've each closed the door to the music business and, from all indications, rarely look over their shoulders. I once asked Willie Nelson about retiring and he said, "I only do two things…sing and play golf. Which one do you want me to give up?"

Which brings up the question: When is the right time to retire? When you hit some magical age like 65? I don't think so. Aside from financial or health considerations, I think retirement should come when what you do for a living isn't fun anymore. Every article I've ever read on the subject stresses that staying active by doing something enjoyable helps to keep a person's mind, body, and spirit alive.

People ask me all the time if I plan to ever retire, and I guess here at the beginning of a new year is a good time to ponder that question. My dad sold his business and quit going to his office on a daily basis when he was my age, but he never did "retire." I've got a new album coming out in a few weeks and a new single being shipped to radio. I've taken my two VHS videos and had them transferred to the DVD format and we'll begin marketing those shortly. I've got some new songs I've co-written that will be released soon plus several others that I need to get into the studio and demo. I've got two new books I'm working on, quite a few songwriting appointments to keep, and a tour schedule for 2005 that is just now beginning to take shape.

I can't retire. I don't have time.

January 13, 2005

Hi Gang:

Well, I'm sure you've noticed the announcement above about our new country album, "The Way I Feel," which is finally about to hit the streets. We're awfully excited about it here, and hope you'll want to add a copy to your collection sometime real soon.

The actual release date is February 1st, but we plan to have a few copies available for our friends who will be aboard the Grand Ole Opry cruise January 22nd. We can begin taking your orders shortly, and as we do on all our new releases, we'll offer the first two hundred copies personally autographed.

I co-wrote all the songs on the CD, and they are all new except for "Whiskey Lullaby." I had not originally intended to include this song, but we've had such tremendous response to the version Kenzie and I have been doing on the Opry that we actually held up the album release until we could record it and get it onto the CD. I hope you'll like it.

We've also been receiving a tremendous initial response to a song called "Him & Me," the title of which you'll notice is also listed on the album cover. This is a song I wrote with Tony Villanueva, formerly of a group called The Derailers, and one that has been playing on XM Satellite Radio for the past couple of months. It's the story of a boy whose father was a truck driver and the memories of his dad that this boy carried into his adult life. We have received incredible response from the XM listeners, many who are truckers, and we'll be releasing this song as the first single from the album shortly.

As you know if you read my last message to you about retirement, I still enjoy writing and recording new music, and I hope this latest effort will please you. Thanks for allowing me to continue to be a part of your record collections after all these years.

I probably won't get to visit with you again in this space until after we return from the Opry cruise on January 30th, so I'll see you then....hopefully rested and tanned.

My best to you all.

January 31, 2005

Hi Gang:

I wish I could say that I arrived home from the Grand Ole Opry cruise well-rested, well-fed, and well-tanned, but I can't. But, then again, two out of three ain't bad.

We had a marvelous time as we always do, pickin' and grinnin' and visiting with country music fans from all over the world. And they literally came from all over the world this year...Australia, New Zealand, Ireland, and many from Canada. We played music, shook hands, posed for pictures, signed autographs...everything one might possibly expect to do on a cruise of this type except lie out in the sun. And why, you ask, did we not make time to lie out in the sun? Oh, we made time all right. There was just very little sun!

The way it was explained to me was that anytime there is a bad storm in the northeastern United States, as weird as it may sound, that storm eventually affects the weather in the Caribbean. Don't ask me to explain it, but while our friends across the Midwest and into New England were battling the snow, we were cruising in much cooler temperatures and beneath much cloudier skies than you might expect. I'm not asking for sympathy. I am simply explaining the lack of my customary January suntan!

The highlight of my trip was being invited to spend a day at Kenny Chesney's incredibly beautiful and secluded home on the island of St. John. I even got to sit in his famous "blue chair" and stare at some of the most gorgeous scenery I have ever experienced. No wonder Kenny goes there to relax and get away from it all. We snapped a few pictures which I hope will turn out good enough to print in our News section later this week. Ironically, at the same time we were loafing in St. John, Kenny's new CD of laid-back Caribbean music, "Be As You Are," was released, and there just happens to be a song in there called "Key Lime Pie" that was written by Kenny, his producer, Buddy Cannon, and yours truly. I hope you'll be listening out for it and will want to add this tasty and very creative album to your collection.

To all the fans who went cruising with us, thanks for some great times and wonderful memories. Sorry I could barely whisper above a whisper on Friday night's guitar pull, but in addition to no suntan, I also managed to catch myself a heckuva cold and sore throat toward the end of the week. To my fellow cruisers from the Opry, Terri Clark, Trace Adkins, Eddie Stubbs, Pete Fisher, and the incomparable Little Jimmy Dickens, thanks for letting me tag along one more time. I'm not going on the Opry cruise next year for the first time in several years, but I know those of you who do go will have fun like always.

I'm going to wait at least two years before going again. I figure surely I'll be over my cold and the sun will be shining by then!

Bill relaxing in Kenny Chesney's "Blue Chair"

February 21, 2005

Hi Folks:

About this time every year, my mailbox begins filling up with letters asking me for information about our annual City Lights Festival in Commerce, Georgia.

A few of the details are still being worked out, but here's what I can tell you so far about our plans for 2005:

The Festival will be held, as always, the third weekend in June, which this year means Thursday June 16th through Saturday June 18th. We will have our annual golf tournament at the Sandy Creek golf course, our Dinner with The Stars at the local civic center, and our big outdoor concert and fireworks display at the football stadium.

And our headline attraction this year will be the incredibly talented and versatile group, Diamond Rio!

James Gregory, "The Funniest Man In America," will lend his comedic talents to the big event, along with the music of Grand Ole Opry star, Jan Howard, Georgia gospel favorites, the Jordans, and of course some guy named Bill Anderson and His Po' Folks Band. Other performing artists and special guests will be announced soon.

Our toll-free phone line will also be open soon to provide ticket information, and I hope you'll keep watching our web site for further details as well. The City Lights Festival is in its ninth year, helping to raise money for the construction of a Performing Arts Center in this small northeast Georgia community about sixty miles from Atlanta where I first started my radio and songwriting career.

Help us spread the word, and we'll see you there!

March 1, 2005

Hi Gang:

And thanks for stopping by our web site.

I'm taking a few days off right now in order to have a little "family time" with my kids and grandkids. Just wanted you to know I'm away from the office in case you were to write me and not get a reply. My batteries need a bit of recharging from time to time, and this is one of those times.

I'll probably have lots of good grandkid stories by the time I get home, but I've got a good one already and I just left.

I was having breakfast with my son, Jamey, and his wife, Beth, and their two boys, Blake and Gabe, over the weekend. Blake, who is two, finished off his pancakes and was in a playful mood. Beth sensed this and asked him, "Blake, what is daddy's name?"

Blake replied, "Daddy's name Jamey."

She then asked, "And what's mommie's name?" Blake answered, "Mommie's name Beth."

Beth then looked at me and asked him, "And what's PawPaw's name?" With a big ole grin on his chubby little face Blake said, "PawPaw's name Whisper!!"

You don't think I was set up for that one by any chance, do you??

Thanks for the many, many orders on our new album, and your kind words about the music we've recorded there. I'll be home and visiting with you again soon.

Steve Wariner had been hired to play bass on a recording with Chet Atkins. Chet listened to him play for awhile and asked, "Did anyone ever tell you that you're a great bass player?"

Steve blushed and admitted that, no, no one ever had.

To which Chet dryly asked, "Ever wonder why?"

March 14, 2005

Hi Gang:

Well, I'm back from my little vacation, well-rested, feisty, and ready to hop back in the ole saddle again.

I had some wonderful family time and several stress-free days away from the daily grind, then returned home to all kinds of exciting news. While I was gone, our song "Whiskey Lullaby" was nominated for four Academy of Country Music awards, including, once again, "Song Of The Year." My co-writer, Jon Randall, and I can only hope the third time is the charm. As you may know, we received this same nomination twice in 2004…at the Grammy Awards and the CMA's, but somebody else took our trophy home both times. The ACM Awards will be on CBS television May 17th from Las Vegas. Cross your fingers.

I also learned while I was away that the duet I recorded with Rustie Blue, "Chip Chip", which is in both her new album and mine, has been nominated for the Vocal Collaboration of the Year by the European Country Music Association. Apparently, Rustie has a big following overseas and tours there often. I don't know much about the E.C.M.A., but if any of their folks happen to read this, thanks a million!

And that's not all. The International Fan Club Organization (IFCO) has informed me that they will be presenting their annual Tex Ritter Award to me during Fan Fair in June. As I understand it, this is a career achievement award presented in the name of America's Most Beloved Cowboy and one of my true friends and heroes, the late, great Tex Ritter. What an honor this will be! The list people who have won it before me reads like a Who's Who of country music.

I've said many times over the years that I never got into this business to win awards, but it's still awfully nice when your name pops up for one. Or two. Or three.

I'm starting to think perhaps I should leave town more often!

March 22, 2005

Hi Gang:

And thanks for stopping by our web site.

Whether this is your first visit or you're one of our regulars, I hope you know you are always welcome here. As welcome, in fact, as the first breath of spring!

I never think of spring arriving that I don't think of my dear friend, Minnie Pearl. Miss Minnie used to talk about one of her "fellers", and she'd say, "He told me I looked like a breath of spring. Actually, what he said was, I looked like the end of a long, hard winter!"

From what I see on the weather reports, some of you are still experiencing the end of a long, hard winter, but the calendar says it's spring just the same. Whatever your thoughts turn to this time of year, I hope they are good ones.

One quick note from here: I told you a few weeks ago that Diamond Rio would be headlining our 9th Annual City Lights Festival in Commerce, Georgia, the third weekend in June, and they will be. However, we have made one small change in the proceedings for this year. The big outdoor concert with Diamond Rio will be on Thursday night June 16th and our golf tournament and Dinner With The Stars will flip-flop with the concert and be held on Friday June 17th. Many of you come in for the entire weekend anyway, so hopefully this small change won't inconvenience anybody. Tickets for the 3-day festival go on sale next week, and for more information you are invited to phone 1-XXX-XXX-XXXX. And be watching this space as more performers are added to the schedule. It's going to be one of our biggest and best festivals yet.

Thanks for all your help and support and kind words about our new album. Copies been flying out of my office about as fast as we can get them in, and for that all of us are grateful.

Have a joyous Easter season, and my best to you all.

March 28, 2005

Hi Gang:

Well, I've got some good news and some not-so-good news.

The good news is that I'm about to be on television again all over the country. The not-so-good part is that you may have to stay up until two or three o'clock in the morning in order to see me!

I've just taped an "infomercial"....you know, one of those thirty-minute commercials that they run in the wee hours. It looks like a regular program only we're trying to sell you something. But, in this case, it's something that I know a lot of you want anyhow.

Remember the video series we did a few years ago called "Country's Family Reunion?" Well, for the first time, these wonderful shows have been put onto digitally-mastered DVD's, and we're now offering nine of them for your enjoyment. These DVDs contain over 130 performances, a total of over 16-hours of songs and stories, from some of country music's greatest all-time legends. Many are by stars who are no longer with us.

Can you imagine sitting in your living room and having one more visit from Boxcar Willie, Skeeter Davis, Grandpa Jones, Chet Atkins, Johnny Russell, and so many more? Well, you can do just that with this incredible DVD collection.

If you see the infomercial, it will bring back memories like you cannot imagine. If you go to bed early, though, you can still find out all about it by calling 1-XXX-XXX-XXXX or visiting the web site at www.cfrvideos.com.

So many people ask me if we're going to film some more of these wonderful reunion visits, and the answer I received from our producer, Larry Black, is that we certainly are…if these DVDs sell as well as we hope. Please help us pass the word. But don't lose too much sleep trying to catch me on TV. I look better on the radio anyhow.

April 6, 2005

Hi Gang:

Well, we have finally put the finishing touches on the talent lineup for our 9th annual City Lights Festival down in my adopted hometown of Commerce, Georgia. It's taken awhile, but I'm as excited about this year's Festival as I've ever been.

As previously announced, the supergroup Diamond Rio will headline our big outdoor concert at Tiger Stadium on Thursday night June 16th at 7 p.m. I'll be there, too, along with my entire Po' Folks Band and local gospel favorites, The Jordans. The show will be followed as always by our gigantic fireworks display.

Friday morning June 17th we'll host our annual golf tournament at the Sandy Creek Golf Course, and Friday night we'll serve up the big Dinner With The Stars at the Civic Center downtown.

In addition to a marvelous, home-cooked, southern-style meal, dinner guests will be entertained "the cowboy way" by the incredibly talented Riders In The Sky. Joining Ranger Doug, Too Slim, Woody Paul, and Joey the Cowpolka King in the spotlight will be one of the loveliest and sweetest singing bluegrass-styled singers in the world today, Miss Melonie Cannon.

I can hardly wait for a night of southern food topped off with western and hill-country music! Does it get any better? I don't think so.

Ticket information for any and all of the Festival events can be obtained by calling our toll-free number at 1-XXX-XXX-XXXX.

I hope lots of you will make your plans to come to Commerce this summer. Last year, we had visitors from 17-states. Let's try and top that in 2005. Commerce is easy to reach, just off Interstate 85 about halfway between Atlanta and Greenville, South Carolina.

We'll see you there!!

April 13, 2005

Hi Gang:

If you were watching the CMT Video Awards Monday night, you heard winner after winner say how much it meant to them to win an award voted on by the fans.

That's also true for those of us who stand on the sidelines and have more than a passing interest in the awards. I wasn't nominated for anything personally, but naturally I wanted to see the video for the song I co-wrote, "Whiskey Lullaby", win in the categories where it was nominated. It did win two out of the three, and for those of you who might have voted for it, I thank you.

Did you know that in the beginning there were no plans to even do a video on that song? Brad Paisley said, and everyone agreed, that the song told the story on its own. But when Rick Schroeder came up with his marvelous treatment of the story and put it onto film, it gave our song a whole new meaning for a lot of people. In particular, it cleared up the confusion over the line about putting the bottle to the head and pulling the trigger. I was happy to see Rick's work acknowledged by your voting him Video Director of the Year.

Record companies, artists, and others within the creative community often debate the value of a video versus the costs involved in making and producing one. I've often wondered how I would have felt about videos had they been in vogue back when my records were riding the charts. There is no doubt but what they have helped reshape the way we listen to the music.

And to quote Ferlin Husky's alter-ego, Simon Crum, "By Ned, I think they're here to stay!"

Overheard on Music Row: "The music business is an itch in the roof of your mouth that can best be scratched with a pistol."

April 19, 2005

Hi Gang:

It was brought to my attention via an e-mail I received this week that I haven't mentioned my radio shows on XM Satellite Radio in this space lately. This particular letter-writer was not familiar with XM at all and asked, "What channel is it and how do I tune in?"

XM is one of two radio services that reaches its listeners via satellite and can be heard all over the hemisphere. It's a subscription service, meaning that you pay a small monthly fee in order to receive nearly 200 channels of digital quality and largely commercial-free radio. For more information, you can go to www.xmradio.com and check it out.

I host a show called "Bill Anderson Visits With The Legends" on XM Channel 10 which is called the America channel. It is an hour-long show (sometimes I get windy and it lasts for 90-minutes!) where, as the name implies, I sit and talk and laugh and play music (both live and recorded) by some of the greatest names in country music. My guests over the past three years have included George Jones, Willie Nelson, Kenny Rogers, Dolly Parton, Merle Haggard, and just about every other country legend you can name. Our show airs a minimum of four times each week. One of the last true legendary country artists to be on my show is Loretta Lynn, and my ninety-minute visit with her will begin airing in May. As of now, the original airing is set for Sunday May 8th at 5 p.m. Eastern. The initial encores will be May 10th at 6 a.m. Eastern, May 12th at 7 p.m. Eastern, May 13th at 8 a.m. Eastern, and May 14th at 2 p.m. Eastern.

XM is available on a free three-day trial via the internet, and the company has recently signed an agreement with AOL to provide some of its programming as well. Again, more details are available through the XM web site.

If you're not already an XM subscriber, you might want to look into it. Six of their channels are devoted to the various genres of country music, and you hear a much wider variety of songs and artists than on most regular radio stations. Just be sure you get an XM radio with a strong volume control....so you can turn it up and hear me whisper!

Dolly Parton

Kris Kristofferson

Moe Bandy

Barbara Mandrell

Ray Stevens

Pat Boone

Rhonda Vincent

Glen Campbell

Kelly Lang,
T.G. Sheppard and
Helen Cornelius

Aaron Tippin

Gene Watson

Donna Fargo

XM Radio Show Producer,
Roxanne Atwood and
Mel Haggard

April 28, 2005

Hi Gang:

The question I have probably been asked more than any other over the
past few months has been, "How did you and Jon Randall come to write
'Whiskey Lullaby'?"

If you've wondered that and never heard or read the answer, you might
want to check out the current edition (May 9th) of Country Weekly
magazine and read the column, "Story Behind The Song." It tells it like
it is. Or like it was.

I continue to be amazed at the reaction our little song has received. By
the time most of you read this, it will have been honored in Beverly Hills,
California, by the Entertainment Industries Council and given its prestigious Prism Award. That is an award, according to the EIC, "recognizing
the accurate depiction of drug, alcohol, and tobacco use and addiction in
film, television, interactive, music, video, and comic book entertainment.
The Prism Awards were established in 1997 and honor productions that
are not only powerfully entertaining, but realistically show substance
abuse and addiction."

There is only one award given in the music category, and that includes
all genres of music. There is only one award given in the music video
category, and that, too, includes all genres of music. "Whiskey Lullaby"
will have won them both.

On May 5th, Music Row magazine in Nashville will honor us with their
"Song Of The Year" award. On May 17th, the song, recording, and video
are up for four additional awards at the Academy of Country Music show
in Las Vegas.

Jon and I are both astounded and ever-grateful for these accolades,
especially in light of the fact that we never thought we'd even get the
song recorded. It sat on the shelf for over three years before Brad
Paisley had the nerve to record it and the brilliance to ask Alison Krauss
to sing it with him.

Thanks to them and to you, we have been most richly blessed.

Sunday May 8, 2005

Hi Gang:

It's funny the things you think about on a day like Mothers' Day.

I remember how my mom believed for a long time that I'd put down my guitar someday, come back home to Georgia, and get a real job, but she never once encouraged me to do so. It was my dream, and she gave me the freedom to chase it.

She never understood how her 19-year old son could sit on the rooftop of a three-story building in a town of four-thousand people and write about "the bright array of city lights as far as I can see…"

She wondered what kinds of friends I was making in Nashville when, not long after my arrival in Music City, I showed up back on her doorstep at six o'clock one morning with a buddy and two large laundry bags full of dirty clothes. Instead of questioning us, she cooked our breakfast and spent all day washing and drying dirty socks, underwear, and blue jeans for me and this wacko guy named Roger Miller. After we'd slept all day, she cooked our dinner, gave us both a big hug, and sent us on our way back to Nashville.

She spent much of her life convincing me that the greatest Mothers' Day present I ever gave her was the Sunday afternoon I took her to Ponce de Leon Park to see the Atlanta Crackers play baseball.

She never quite understood why I wrote "Mama Sang A Song" about someone who couldn't sing a lick. I tried to tell her the song was about her heart and not about her voice, but I'm not sure the beauty of that truth ever fully registered.

She told me time and again that it didn't matter how big a star I became…or how successful I was in the public eye…I was still, and would always be, her little "curly-headed boy." And when people would say to her, "Mrs. Anderson, you must be so proud of Bill," she'd simply smile and say, "I was proud of him the day he was born."

I was sitting in the middle of her living room floor not long before she passed away when she told me, "I've had a wonderful life. Don't be sad when I'm gone."

I always tried to mind my mother, but I've had a tough time with that one. Especially today.

I miss you, Mom. Happy Mother's Day.

May 18, 2005

Hi Gang:
I don't know the statistics, but I'd venture to say that the vast majority of people who come to Las Vegas, the gambling capital of the world, hope to become winners while they are here but, in fact, end up leaving town as losers.

Not so for the Academy of Country Music following their 40th Anniversary Awards Show here Tuesday night. The ACM and country music as a whole, are leaving this desert metropolis as big winners indeed.

The Academy, born in southern California in the mid-sixties as a west coast alternative to the Nashville-based Country Music Association, cleverly employed the latest in satellite technology to display the global reach of today's country music, showcasing Toby Keith performing for our military forces in Iraq and a sleepy, but obviously very happy, Keith Urban accepting two ACM awards live from Belfast, Northern Ireland.

From my vantage point on the floor inside the convention center at the Mandalay Hotel & Resort, there was a long list of winners. From Lee Ann Womack's stone-country performance which earned the first standing ovation of the evening to Garth Brooks' touching tribute to his friend and idol, the late Chris Ledoux, it was an evening of successes.

I'd be lying if I said Jon Randall and I hadn't hoped to win Song of the Year for our composition, "Whiskey Lullaby" (I had a great acceptance speech ready!), but to see our song win in two of the four categories in which it was nominated (Video and Vocal Collaboration) was special enough. Thanks, Brad and Alison and Rick one more time!

One of my fan club members, Billie Hicklin from North Carolina, won a nationwide contest which afforded her and another of our members, Betty Parrish, a free trip to the celebration and all its related festivities. When I last saw them in the hotel casino shortly after midnight, their tired feet and smiling faces were parked in front of the penny slot machines!

Las Vegas losers? From where I stood, there wasn't one in sight.

May 25, 2005

Hi Gang:

This time last week I was writing you from the strip in Las Vegas where the skies were sunny and the temperature was on its way up to 97-degrees. Today, I am writing from the foggy coast of Maine where it's raining and the temperature won't get out of the sixties. You probably think I'm crazy for making such a trade, but you know what? The rocky shoreline of Maine, with its myriad of inlets and islands, energizes me and stirs my creative spirit like no other place I have ever found.

Lots of other writers, artists, painters, etc., must feel the same way, because this area is a haven for many who make their living from the arts. I won't divulge any names or point out any hideaway locations, but I'll confess to being one among them. Ever since I first came here on vacation about ten years ago, Maine has been like a magnet pointed directly at my soul. I'm here this time with my songwriting buddy, Don Cook, and in the two and a half days since we hit the area we've started and completed three new songs, shared a jillion laughs, and made a serious dent in the lobster and blueberry population of the state. Unfortunately, the real world beckons, and I have to leave and head for home tomorrow. Jimmy Dean always referred to Maine as a "sweet place" when we used to come here and relax on his yacht, the "Big Bad John." I agree, and I hope to head this way again later this summer. But I've been thinking it over. As much as I love it here, I'll put a good old fashioned Las Vegas wager on the fact that I'll head south and leave Maine to the natives when the snow starts to fly this winter.

June 2, 2005

Hi Gang:

The world of advertising has always fascinated me. There seems to be no end to the methods and strategies companies are willing to use in an attempt to have us purchase their particular services or products. I remember as a young boy, in the days long before jet airplanes and a sky full of vapor trails, when small airplanes would write white, fluffy messages against the bright blue summer skies. I'd sit for hours watching a pilot carefully sketching out the letters "P-e-p-s-i", even down to dotting the i. But I honestly don't remember ever drinking a Pepsi because of it.

Tattoos are big things today, and we've all been reading lately of people having commercial messages tattooed on their various body parts. The pregnant woman who allowed a baby-goods store to purchase space on her bare and ever-enlarging tummy gets my vote as the most creative. Wonder if she'd have done that, though, had she been expecting in Maine during December?

My sister, Mary, and I got to laughing on the phone not long ago about a time when we were kids and a big advertising campaign hit our hometown: "White rain is coming to Atlanta!" screamed every newspaper headline and billboard in sight. Mary was beside herself. "I've never seen white rain," she'd cry excitedly. "I can't wait to see what it looks like!"

Well, as fate would have it, on the very day that Atlanta was to be drenched by this spectacular "white rain", our parents decided we needed to go visit our grandparents in Griffin, some forty miles to the south. "But the white rain isn't going to fall in Griffin!" Mary screamed. "It says it's coming to Atlanta!" Mama and Daddy pushed her kicking and screaming into the back seat of our '41 Chevrolet and quickly locked the doors.

Mary learned a lot about the tricks of the advertising trade that day when we got home and she found out that the "white rain" that had been forecast for Atlanta was simply the introduction of a new shampoo! Advertisers have had a hard time convincing her of anything ever since!

Happy Birthday today, Sis. I love you,

June 6, 2005

Question: What time is it?

Clues: The outdoor temperatures are on the rise, the humidity is higher than it's been all year, there's at least a 30% chance of rain every day, and there are more out-of-state license plates on the streets of Nashville than ever before.

Answer: It's Fan Fair time!!

Ooops, I'm sorry. It's CMA Music Festival time. They changed the name a few years ago to get rid of the "stigma," but for those of us who have been here since the begining, it will probably always be Fan Fair. Long-standing habits die slow.

Whatever you want to call it, if you're already in town for the week-long festivities or if you're at home packing for the trip, may I extend a hearty welcome to Music City on behalf of myself and the more than a million-plus people who call this area home. As entertainers, we spend much of our time throughout the year traveling to your hometowns, and while the doors to Nashville are open year 'round, this is our moment to shine and welcome you here in the largest numbers of the year. Have fun and enjoy.

My personal schedule for the week is posted on the Tour page of our web site, and I invite you to check it out and come by our booth, to our fan club dinner, to the Grand Ole Opry, or to any one of the other places where I'll be appearing during the week. I've been to every one of these gatherings except one since its inception back in the seventies, and I never tire of seeing old friends and making new ones.

I'm especially looking forward to seeing the little girl who came up to me last year and asked for my autograph. "I don't know who you are," she said, "but my granny likes old people!"

I'm sorry to say I haven't gotten any younger, but maybe this year her granny will at least tell her who I am.

June 15, 2005

Hi Gang:
Well, there's one in my rear view mirror and one staring me in the face through the windshield of a tour bus. It's Country Music Festival time for sure.

We just finished with the CMA Music Festival in Nashville, and what a week it was. They say it was the largest of the 34 Festivals (formerly known as Fan Fair) in history, and it was the 33rd one that I have personally been able to attend.

We've got lots of pictures from the Festival in the News section, so I hope while you're visiting our web site that you'll check them out. We don't have a picture yet from the International Fan Club Organization show on Tuesday night at the Ryman, but suffice it to say it was a wonderful night for yours truly. IFCO presented me with their prestigious Tex Ritter Award, which is a career achievement award, and needless to say I was highly honored. Hopefully we'll have some pictures from that event soon.

As I'm writing this, I'm headed to my adopted hometown of Commerce, Georgia, for our 9th annual City Lights Festival, and it should be an incredible weekend as well. Diamond Rio headlines our big outdoor show Thursday night June 16th and Riders In The Sky along with Melonie Cannon will provide the entertainment at our Dinner With The Stars on Friday. If you're anywhere near Commerce (about halfway between Atlanta and Greenville, South Carolina) I hope you'll come by and partake of the food, friendship, and fun.

It's an incredible time of year filled with lots of pickin' and grinnin'. Now if I can just manage to work in a little sleepin'

June 28, 2005

Hi Gang:

At the end of this year's CMA Music Festival, the event formerly known as Fan Fair, a respected and well-known country music journalist wrote that he felt there might have been two different audiences participating in this year's festivities.

I am paraphrasing here, but he said he observed that one group, comprised mainly of older, more heavy-set fans, seemed to be primarily focused on obtaining autographs from the stars at the Convention Center. A more youthful, trimmer and more well-tanned group, he opined, preferred to party-down at the Riverfront Stages concert area.

The following week at our City Lights Festival in Commerce, I encountered an attractive, 23-year old real estate agent dancing alongside the stage as Diamond Rio performed for a mostly seated adult audience. I overheard this obviously disappointed young lady say, "I've never been to a concert where people sat down before!"

Are there really, in fact, two different country music audiences these days? There well may be, but I hope not. Let me tell you why:

At a recent performance of the Tuesday Night Opry, I stood before one of the greatest crowds I have ever seen in the Grand Ole Opry House. Every seat was full, and they were selling standing room only tickets at the door. There were older people, young people, heavy-set people, thin people - all seated side by side and all cheering for the music. And who was making the music? Porter Wagoner, Trace Adkins, Jack Greene, Aaron Tippin, Dierks Bentley, Del McCourey, Bill Anderson, and George Jones. Oh yes, and George's daughter, Georgette, who was making her first ever appearance on the Opry stage. Has there ever been a more diverse group of entertainers on the same bill?

There was traditional country music bouncing off the walls right alongside today's modern country sounds with a touch of bluegrass thrown in for good measure. Did the older people only applaud the older artists? Of course not. Did the younger people only applaud the new music? Are you kidding? Porter left the stage to one of the loudest ovations I've ever heard, but then so did Trace and Jack and Aaron and Dierks and Del and Bill and George and Georgette. The older fans were exposed to some youngsters they had possibly never seen before. The

younger fans got to hear some of the legendary sounds that have made this art form what it is. And unless I'm highly mistaken, over forty-five hundred people left the building feeling as though they had just spent one of the most memorable nights of their lives.
Isn't that as it should be?

On stage at the Grand Ole Opry

June 20, 2005

Hi Gang:

With all my traveling and "festival hopping" these past couple of weeks, I let Fathers' Day slip up on me. Belated good wishes to all the fathers among us.

I was able to be with two of my three children on Sunday, having been with my third earlier in the week. But it was the memories of my own dad that occupied much of my mind.

I've often wondered how things might have been between the two of us had computers come along a bit earlier in his life. Due to my hectic schedule and his, we would sometimes be forced to go quite some time between visits and telephone conversations, but we burned up the U.S. mail.

Every time one of us would see something in a newspaper or a magazine that we thought the other would be interested in or enjoy, we'd clip it out, lick a postage stamp, and send it to the other. We exchanged everything from sports columns and jokes to cartoons, advertisements, and obituary notices, most of it probably meaningless to anyone other than us. But when I'd go to the mailbox and see an envelope with his return address on it, it was invariably the first one I would open. Imagine if he had been able to master e-mail. We'd have been so busy copying, pasting, and writing back and forth that I'd probably have never written another song nor he another insurance policy.

I miss you, Dad, more than I could ever have imagined. Happy Fathers Day a little late…and Happy Birthday five days early.

Bluegrass legend, the late Jimmy Martin, was venting about the state of bluegrass music. "I tell you what's wrong with it," he offered. "There's too much jealousy and stupidy."

July 5, 2005

Hi Gang:
I hope everyone had a safe and happy 4th of July weekend and you're all rested up from the holiday. I know you can't wait to get back to work again.

Yeah…sure!
You might have noticed over the weekend, or when you signed onto our web site this time, that we've been working hard putting together a special "Christmas In July" sale on some of our selected merchandise items. This is the first of many monthly specials we plan to run for the rest of 2005, and I hope we'll have some offers that you'll want to take advantage of. It's our way of trying to say "thank you" for being some of the best fans and friends in the world.
You'll also notice our long-promised DVD is finally ready, and I hope you'll be wanting to add that to your collection as well. If you order this month, it comes with a free poster. Take that big poster out in your garden, and you won't need to put up a scarecrow this year!!
The DVD is made up of the two VHS tapes that I have previously released, "Bill Anderson's Video Scrapbook" and "Bill Anderson Live", so you may have already seen some of the material, but the DVD quality and portability make this much more of a keepsake item than ever before. With a price tag of only $19.95 for over two-hour's worth of music and entertainment, I hope you'll want one for yourself and perhaps an additional one for that special someone on your gift list.
As always, thanks for stopping by to see us, and come back soon and often. And if any of you have any pull with the weatherman, tell him to send a little rain to Nashville. My lawn sure could use it.
Thanks,

July 19, 2005

Hi Folks:

And welcome to our web site. I appreciate your dropping by, and hope you'll stay long enough to catch up on everything's that going on in Whisper World!

If you are a first-time visitor, you might be interested to know that ever so often I write little messages in this space talking about everything from soup to nuts. In my last message, I ended it by asking any of our readers who might have a little pull with the weatherman to please see if they could get some rain sent toward Nashville. My lawn was getting awfully dr

Well, I should have remembered my Mama's advice from years ago. "Be careful what you ask for, wish for, or pray for, son, because you're liable to get it." Mama would be disappointed in me for ignoring her warning, but she'd be proud of the results.

You see, my dry and cracked lawn is now a gigantic quagmire.

Somebody out there has more pull with the weatherman than they ought to have. And, according to the forecast, the rain isn't supposed to let up for any length of time anytime soon.

But hang on a minute. This may just have a good side. We've obviously got some readers out there with lots of pull. Forget the weatherman. Do any of you have any influence over a Hummer dealer, a rich old man with lots and lots of money, the people who are in charge of the country music charts, et cetera, et cetera, et cetera????

The possibilities here are endless!

A song title overheard at Fan Fair: "The Last Word In Cousin Is Sin."

Bluegrass great Sonny Osborne who is now retired from the music business: "I saw too many nights turn into day without a bed involved."

July 27, 2005

Hi Gang:
I've written in this space before that the greatest compliment a
songwriter or a singer can be paid is for someone to say, "You
must have written (or sung) that song just for me."
"You said in that song exactly what I was feeling, but didn't know
how to put into words. You put it into words for me."
I was reminded of that all over again last week when I received an
e-mail from a lady in Oklahoma telling me how the song, "Peanuts &
Diamonds", which I recorded years ago, touched her life.
The song (written by Bobby Braddock) tells the story of a poor cowboy
from Ft. Worth who falls in love with a rich woman from Dallas. He can
only afford to give her peanuts but wishes he could give her diamonds.
She sits alone in her mansion with her diamonds and wishes they were his
peanuts. The fan who wrote me said this song mirrored her life exactly,
and that the cowboy from Ft. Worth was "the one who got away."
Her e-mail caused me to recall another letter I received many years ago
from a man in Louisiana. He told me that he had been driving himself out
into a secluded place in the bayou country with every intention of
committing suicide when my recording of "Five Little Fingers" came on his
car radio…a song where a man thinks he has nothing left to live for until
he feels the touch of his daughter's five little fingers on his hand. He
realizes he has this precious child who needs him, and he clings to that
knowledge in his darkest hour. The letter-writer told me that my song
caused him to realize how selfish he had been, and how his life had been
changed from that moment on.
My grandfather, a Methodist minister, told me shortly before he died that I
was in a position to reach more people with one song than he had reached
with every sermon he had ever preached. I didn't fully
understand it at the time, but he was right.
Sometimes it's an overwhelming feeling, not to mention an
awesome responsibility.

90

August 8, 2005

Hi Gang:

Thanks for stopping by our web site. It's always good to have you. You've probably noticed at the top of this page that we are selling our audio cassette tapes for the incredibly low price of just $5.00 throughout the month of August. Why? Because, frankly, we are overstocked, and we are finding on our concert dates and through our mail order business that most people don't buy their music on cassette tapes anymore.

Some of you are probably like me in that you remember when cassettes were the newest and most hip way to listen to your favorite music. They were small and extremely portable, perfect for that Walkman or the tape deck in the car or truck. They were much less cumbersome than their predecessor, the dreaded 8-track tape. Those things would stop in the middle of a song to switch tracks, the same song would repeat two or three times on the same package, and they were always breaking or getting chewed to shreds inside the player.

But now their handy-dandy little replacements have given 'way to compact discs, and even the CD's themselves are in danger of being put out to pasture by MP3's, iPod's, and all kinds of things we've probably not yet heard of.

Do the cassettes still sound good? Sure. Perhaps you get a little tape-noise you don't hear on a digital recording, but much like the old vinyl albums, some folks think the overall sound is warmer and more honest. All the hits are there, the original artwork, the songs in their entirety, and you'll never be able to beat the price. Plus, it's only about twenty weeks or so until Christmas, and cassette tapes make great little stocking-stuffers.

Don't get me wrong. Please. I'm not trying to sell you anything. I'm just trying to be helpful….and to clear out some storage space at my office!

August 22, 2005

Hi Gang:

You know, not everybody who contributes to the field of country music is a star who gets to stand in the spotlight and soak up the applause and the accolades. I've often felt that the background musicians, those who play the music behind the star on his or her recordings and/or stand in the shadows behind the featured performers on stage, are the unsung (no pun intended) heroes of our profession.

We lost three of our industry's most outstanding musicians within the past week or so, and each will be sorely missed.

Rufus Thibidoux was quite possibly the best Cajun-styled fiddler who ever graced a country music stage. I recall once being on tour with my buddy, Roger Miller, down in Louisiana, and remember how Roger could hardly wait for our own show to be over so we could leave the fancy auditorium downtown and drive to the outskirts of town to hear Rufus playing with a Cajun band in a crowded, clapboard honky-tonk. It was my introduction to Rufus' genius on his instrument, and I remained a fan throughout the rest of his life. He often played with Jimmy C. Newman at the Opry, and the show seemed to have an extra bit of sparkle on the nights that he was there.

I first met steel guitar genius Hal Rugg when he was in the staff band at the old Flame Theater Café (a fancy description of a glorified honky-tonk) in Minneapolis. Hal played pedal steel in the staff band along with a young Jimmy Colvard on lead guitar, providing the Flame with the best one-two musical punch outside of Nashville. (Jimmy would later play the signature acoustical guitar licks on my recording of "Golden Guitar") Both ended up in Music City, displaying their craft both in the recording studios and on countless stages worldwide. Hal probably played steel on as many hit records as any other steel guitar player in history, and I know for sure he told me as many jokes backstage as anyone I was ever around. I will always remember his talent and the smiles he brought to my face.

Vassar Clements probably came closer than Rufus or Hal to being regarded as a "star", although he got his start playing fiddle behind Bill Monroe while he was still in his teens. Put a fiddle in his hands, and Vassar could explode with a touch and a passion unmatched in any form or style of music. He was often referred to as a "hillbilly jazz" musician, a compliment of the highest order. One of my favorite interviews as host of the "Legends" show on XM radio came the day Vassar Clements, along with Eddie Stubbs and Buddy Spicher, graced our studio. It was ninety minutes of incredible music and laughter that won't soon be forgotten. Their names may not have been household words, but Rufus, Hal, and Vassar each left an indelible mark on our ears and our hearts. I'm privileged to have been able to call each of them my friend. Mostly, we are ALL privileged because they left us so much wonderful music to treasure and remember.

Bill, Buddy Spicher, Eddie Stubbs and Vassar Clements

September 6, 2005

Hi Gang:
With all the suffering and horror that has been unfolding this past week along our nation's Gulf Coast, the comings and goings of the music business seem awfully minor and trivial.
I simply didn't have the heart to try and write my usual weekly message to you. Like most of you, my eyes have been glued to the TV and my ears to the radio as this most tragic of all tragedies has played out right in front of us. And, like you, I have watched and listened and felt totally helpless.
It's been awfully hard to go on stage and smile.
Hopefully, it won't be long before things will begin to look up and we can all begin to look forward. America is and has always been a resilient nation, and we'll manage somehow to pull together and fight back.
Meantime, my sympathies, condolences, and prayers join yours in going out to all our brothers and sisters who are in pain.
May God bless us all.

Sept. 14, 2005

Hi Gang:
Well, I guess by now most of you have heard that "Whiskey Lullaby" has been nominated again for Song of the Year.
Ever since the nominations were announced, I've been getting e-mails, phone calls, cards, and letters from folks asking me how this could be possible. "How can a song be nominated for Song of the Year two years in a row?" they inquire.
My answer is a simple one: "I don't know.
And that's the truth. I do know that George Jones' "He Stopped Loving Her Today" was a two-time CMA winner back in the eighties, as was Freddie Hart's "Easy Loving" in the seventies. But I don't know the inner

workings of the CMA Awards process well enough to tell you just how it happened.

Lots of folks think we won this award in 2004, but we didn't. "Whiskey Lullaby" won for Vocal Event of the Year and Video of the Year, but not for Song of the Year. So we've got another chance in 2005.

But I'm not about to ask how it happened or why. Somebody might get to investigating and decide to take our nomination away.

So Shhhh!! Mum's the word!

September 19, 2005

I had a once-in-a-lifetime experience this past weekend.

I went home to Georgia for my 50-year high school reunion.

I graduated from Avondale High School, just outside Atlanta, in a class of 114 students. We were always a close-knit group, but we were brought together even more closely when, one week before we were to graduate, our school building caught fire and burned to the ground. Commencement exercises were held on the football field behind the charred remains of what had been my home away from home for five years. (No, I didn't fail a grade…high school started with the 8th grade back then!) The air was filled with the smell of ashes, and what should have been a celebratory time for us all became instead a time of sadness. Some of the diplomas, which had been inside a safe in the principal's office, were singed around the edges, including mine…a permanent reminder of our loss.

But this weekend we didn't dwell on our unhappy graduation night. We celebrated instead the 59 classmates who came together for what will probably be the last time. We lit two dozen candles in memory of the twenty-four members of our class who have gone on before us, and we wondered as to the whereabouts of the eight others we were unable to locate. Mostly though we laughed and told stories and relived memories generated in a much less complicated day and time.

Each member of the class got up following dinner and told a little about themselves…where they're living now, how many kids and grandkids they have, and, for many, the jobs from which they are now retired. When it came my time to speak, it suddenly dawned on me that most of the people in that room had been in the audience that December day in 1952 when I performed in public for the very first time. It was a school talent show, and the Avondale Playboys and I were judged by the applause we received to be the winners of the show. I grew very emotional telling my former classmates that, without any of us having realized it at the time, they were the ones who had given me the first encouragement I ever received to pursue a career in the music business.

The wife of one of my classmates said to me afterward, "I'll bet most people in your position don't go back to their high school reunions." I smiled and replied, "Well, if they don't, they have no idea what they've missed."

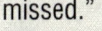

September 28, 2005

Hi Gang!
Have you ever noticed when you're not having the best of days how much an unexpected laugh can cheer you up, relax you, and make you feel better?
Even if the joke is on you?
I had to have a minor medical procedure performed earlier this week and, truth be known, I was a bit edgy about it. I was lying on the hospital operating table just about to be given my sedation when I overheard a nurse talking from over in the far corner of the room.
She was standing at a sink washing her hands, and I really don't think she was talking to anyone in particular. But she was speaking loud enough for me to understand every word.
"Hey," she belted, "somebody out at the desk told me we've got a musician in here!"
That got my attention. I turned my head only to hear her add, "I told 'em, 'Awww, that's no musician. It's just ole Whisperin' Bill'!"
They probably heard me laughing from one end of that hospital to the other. All I could think of was how much my band members would have loved that! And I'll bet when I went under, I had a grin from one side of my face to the other.

October 5, 2005

Hi Gang:
Autumn has always been my favorite time of year.
I love it when the temperatures begin to cool, the humidity begins to fall, and the leaves begin to turn. Not to mention the baseball playoffs that are now underway, the World Series that's just around the corner, and

both the college and professional football seasons that are in full swing. Pumpkins and Halloween decorations already dot the sides of the roads, and before we know it, we'll be focusing our attention on Thanksgiving turkeys and family get-togethers.

I'm in the midst of taking a few days off to travel and enjoy some of nature's beauty and serenity. When I return, it will be time to celebrate the Grand Ole Opry's 80th birthday, time to dress up for the annual songwriters' and performers' banquets around Nashville, and this year, for the first time ever, time to get ready to go to New York for the CMA Awards and Grand Ole Opry night at Carnegie Hall.

I hope you are enjoying this marvelous season wherever you are. For me, it simply doesn't get any better than this.

October 12, 2005

Hi Gang:

I guess most of you know that this coming weekend we'll be celebrating the 80th Anniversary of the Grand Ole Opry.

Actually, the Opry was first broadcast on November 25, 1925 (no, I was NOT there!), but because the weather in Nashville can be so unpredictable that time of year, the annual celebration itself was moved forward to October several years ago. You know, kind of like we celebrate all our holidays on Mondays now, whether the event we are commemorating actually took place on that date or not.

Most people, places, or things that survive for eighty years are considered "old," but I was thinking this morning that's not really true of the Opry. Sure, there's a few of us who have been hanging our hats there for quite a few years, but the Opry has managed to stay "young" by opening its doors in recent years to the younger stars of country music as well as us "old timers." Their music isn't exactly like ours, but then ours wasn't exactly like that of the ones who preceded us either.

I often hear complaints that some of the younger artists don't have the heartfelt commitment to the Opry that many of my generation did, and in some cases that's probably true. But many of them do. And for that reason, I think the Opry stands a good chance of being around for another eighty years.

As Mel McDaniel wrote and Conway Twitty sang, the Opry is "The Grandest Lady Of Them All."

Happy Birthday, Sweetheart....even if it is a month early!

October 18, 2005

Hi Gang:

I'm sure you know as well or better than I what an incredible artist Garth Brooks is and has been for many years. I want to spend a few minutes of your time telling you what a marvelous human being he is as well.

Garth went into a self-imposed retirement mode a few years ago, and, by his own choice, virtually disappeared off the show business radar. When he heard about the Grand Ole Opry's 80th birthday celebration last weekend, however, he wanted to come to Nashville to be a part of it. Not to come out of his retirement but to "honor the Opry."

He could have walked on that stage in front of a national television audience Saturday night and sung any number of his million-selling hit songs. Most people, myself included, expected that was exactly what he would do. But he didn't do that at all.

First, he and Steve Wariner teamed up on the hit they wrote together, "Longneck Bottle." Then Garth insisted that Little Jimmy Dickens, Porter Wagoner, and myself join him on stage for a medley of classic country music duets. Instead of Garth's fans hearing him sing "The Dance", "Friends In Low Places", or "Two Pina Coladas", they heard him join Jimmy on "May The Bird Of Paradise Fly Up Your Nose." He sang "Bright Lights And Country Music" with me, and "The Green, Green Grass Of Home" with Porter. Then we topped it all off with a group sing on

"Y'all Come."

Most artists, given that same opportunity, would have opted to further their own cause in some way. But Garth Brooks is not, nor has he ever been, "most artists." He is an exceptionally kind, caring and giving human being.

"You guys have always made me feel like one of you," he whispered to me in the midst of a big bear hug backstage after the show. This from a man who has sold more country music albums and more concert tickets than anyone in the history of our art form. He stepped back from the glare of the spotlight and allowed three of us "old-timers" to step in. Without his generosity, we most likely would not have had that chance. Pardon my language, but Garth Brooks, you are one helluva man.

Garth Brooks, Porter Wagoner, Bill and Little Jimmy Dickens

October 31, 2005

Hi Gang & Happy Halloween:
I met a man a few nights ago who told me his occupation was "gun collector."
I asked him how he got into the business of collecting guns and he said, "It was a hobby that got out of hand."
I had to laugh. "That's the same way I got into the music business," I told him. "I've spent more than forty years making a living with a 'hobby that got out of hand'!"
I think most people who are professional songwriters, musicians, and performers would probably say the same thing. Music started out in their lives simply as something they enjoyed. Had they not become accomplished enough to make a living from their music, they would have continued to write, play, and sing music simply for the love of it. I've often shared some advice I once read in a newspaper: "Find something you like doing so much that you'd do it for nothing. Then learn to do it so well they'll pay you, and you've got it made." I've maintained for years that the most fortunate people in the world are those who make a living doing something they love.
I never thought of it quite this way before, but I think I'll spend some of my future energy encouraging young people to develop a healthy hobby. Then perhaps, if they're lucky, their hobby, too, will "get out of hand."

Conway Twitty after once watching videos on VH1 and MTV: "If I had known rock 'n roll was going to turn out like this, I'd have never invented it."

My own personal favorite letter from a would-be songwriter telling me about a great new song he had composed: "Ain't but one person in the world can sing it," he wrote, "and that's George Jones or Merle Haggard."

November 8, 2005

Hi Gang:
A week ago I celebrated my sixty-eighth birthday.
And when I say "celebrated", I mean "celebrated!" And not for any
reason that you might think.
It all goes back to my childhood. When I was about twelve or thirteen
years old, somebody gave me a Ouija board. Some of you may not know
what a Ouija board is, but as best as I can describe it, it's an old-fash-
ioned game where you "ask" the board a question and it supposedly
answers. You rest your fingertips atop a small wooden cursor, and this
object allegedly moves by itself across a wooden board full of letters and
numbers, eventually spelling or pointing out the answer to your question.
It has no scientific basis whatsoever, and is probably a first cousin to
witchcraft.
Anyhow, my buddy, Wayne Turner, who was two days younger than I,
decided one afternoon to ask the Ouija board how old we were going to
be when we died. The board told Wayne he was going to live to be
eighty-three years old. When he died in his fifties, I should have known
it was all a hoax.
BUT...the board told me I was going to live to be sixty-seven. For the
past year, I have been avoiding stepping on cracks in the sidewalk,
dodging ladders, black cats, and been especially careful not to break any
mirrors, walk out in front of any moving vehicles, or slip on any banana
peelings. Not that I really believed a stupid old board, of course, but just
to be on the safe side.
Now do you understand what I mean when I say I "celebrated" my
sixty-eighth birthday? I made it! I don't intend to relax my vigil anytime
soon, but it sure is nice to know I have a little breathing room!
Oh, and by the way, thanks to each of you who sent birthday greetings
my way, even without your knowing the full significance of the occasion.
I read each and every one I received, and I appreciated them all.

November 14, 2005

Hi Gang:

And thanks for stopping by our website.

By the time you read this, I will be in New York City to take part in the country music "invasion" of the Big Apple.

I'll be part (although a small part) of the Grand Ole Opry night at Carnegie Hall on Monday, and then anxiously awaiting the fate of "Whiskey Lullaby" in the Song of the Year category at the CMA Awards inside Madison Square Garden on Tuesday.Like a lot of people in our industry, I have mixed feelings about the awards show leaving Nashville, but I'll reserve final judgment until all is said and done and we see what the long-term benefits turn out to be. I hope you'll be watching on CBS-TV Tuesday night (15th), and I'll look forward to reading and hearing your comments afterward. Oh, and if you want to cross your fingers for our little song, it would be most appreciated!

Grand Ole Opry on Stage at Carnegie Hall

November 17, 2005

Thank You! Thank You! Thank You!

I cannot possibly reply personally to all the e-mails I have received here at our web site following the CMA Awards telecast on Tuesday night, but I do want you to know that I've read (and I am continuing to read) your wonderful messages of congratulations following our song, "Whiskey Lullaby" winning Song of the Year for 2005. In my last message in this space I asked you to cross your fingers for us. There must have been an awful lot of crossed fingers all around the world, and again all I know to say is "thank you."

When I get down off Cloud 9 (and back from a quick personal appearance trip to North Dakota!) I'll write more about the entire New York experience. It was quite something...from having the chance to appear on stage at Carnegie Hall right down to tucking that incredible award up under my arm inside Madison Square Garden. They may have to surgically remove this grin from my face!

As we approach the Thanksgiving season, I have so much to be thankful for. Mostly my fans, my friends, my co-workers, Jon, Brad, Alison....everybody who contributed to make this very special dream come true. After more than 45-years in the country music business, I thought I had experienced it all. I hadn't...but right now I feel as though I have.

Thanks again,

Jon Randall

November 21, 2005

Hi Gang:

Last November I wrote in this space that one of my boyhood heroes was a sportswriter in Atlanta named Furman Bisher. When I was a teenager and attempting to be a bit of a sportswriter myself, I wanted to grow up to be him.

Every Thanksgiving he would (and still does, to the best of my knowledge) write a column in the newspaper listing the things he was most thankful for that particular year. With apologies to him for once again borrowing his idea, I've made a third annual list of my own: I'M THANKFUL...

For the sun that came up this morning over the Tennessee hills, and that I was able to get out of bed, make coffee, and be gifted with another day as a small part of God's incredible creation.

I'm thankful for second chances...and third and fourth and fifth chances...allowing us the opportunity to make up for the mistakes we made the first few times around.

I'm thankful for the gift of "Whiskey Lullaby," and the fact that it succeeded in spite of all the obstacles that stood in its way. It sat unrecorded for over three years because people said it was too country, too long, too depressing, and too out-of-step with today's country music. I'm thankful for Brad Paisley, who believed in the song from the moment he first heard it, for his producer, Frank Rogers, who first envisioned the song as a duet, and for Alison Krauss, who was, for those few incredible moments, Brad's perfect duet partner. Most of all I'm thankful for Jon Randall who, unfortunately, had to live much of the song before he and I combined to put it down on paper. I'm thankful for the sun that now shines on his life, proving once again that God's timing is much better than our own.

I'm thankful that I lived long enough to attend my 50-year high school reunion this past September...and for the wonderful friendships and spirits that were refreshed and re-kindled throughout that very special weekend.

I'm thankful for contemporary artists like Martina McBride and LeeAnn Womack who hold to their unwavering faith in traditional country music. And even though Martina says she didn't know I wrote it, I'm thankful she included "Once A Day" among the chestnuts on her marvelous new CD called "Traditions."

105

I'm thankful for the Country's Family Reunion DVD's, and for Larry Black who had the wisdom and the foresight to preserve for the ages some of our industry's most incredible personalities, music, and moments. When the shows were first recorded, they were designed as entertainment. Today they are a piece of history because, sadly, so many of the participants are no longer with us.

I'm thankful for both Nashville and New York, and the marvelous way the two cities came together to celebrate country music this past week. I thought how much my mom and dad would have loved to have been there to see me walk on stage at Carnegie Hall. Later I realized they WERE there, and they had the best seats in the house.

I'm thankful for my sister, Mary, who continues to stand up to the cancer that has ravaged her body but which has not even begun to make a dent in her spirit or her soul. For the thousands of prayers that have been prayed on her behalf, our entire family is incredibly grateful.

I'm thankful for three remarkable children and six delightful grandchildren, each of whom leaves an indelible footprint on my heart every day. And I'm thankful for the memories of Thanksgivings past…the smell of mama's turkey and dressing hot from the oven and the heartfelt blessing my daddy would always say prior to the meal. No one could offer thanks to the Lord for our "many, many blessings" quite like my daddy.

I'm thankful once again for our servicemen and women who, by no choice of their own, must spend Thanksgiving apart from their loved ones this year because they are somewhere helping to insure and protect the freedoms the rest of us too often take for granted.

I'm even thankful for the fellow traveler who walked up to me in the Minneapolis airport two nights after the CMA Awards and said, "My wife HATES 'Whiskey Lullaby'!" I laughed and told him I was glad his wife didn't have a vote.

And I'm thankful for each of you, my fans and my friends, who stopped by my web site today. May we each be renewed by the season and reminded of our many, many blessings…not just at Thanksgiving but on every single day of the year.

Happy Thanksgiving!

November 28, 2005

Hi Gang:

I hope everyone had a wonderful Thanksgiving.

I'm still giving thanks up on Cloud 9 somewhere following our recent trip to New York City for the Grand Ole Opry show at Carnegie Hall and the 39th Annual CMA Awards. Much has been written and said about the occasion already, but I have a few thoughts, observations, and memories that you won't see anywhere else:

When they announced that the next award would be presented for "Song of the Year" I turned to Jon Randall and shook his hand. "I hope we win," I said, "but no matter what happens, it's been a helluva ride." He agreed, and added with a mischievous grin, "I hope we win for YOUR sake. At your age, you need to win one NOW!"

When Willie Nelson tore open the blue sheet of paper he held in his hand all I heard him say was, "The award for Song of the Year goes to Whis...." I assume he went on to say "....key Lullaby" but I couldn't hear him above the pounding of my heart.

Big, deep-voiced Trace Adkins, who has, in a relatively short amount of time, gone from singing in suburban Nashville honky-tonks to becoming a major force in today's country music, stood next to me looking out from the stage at the magnificence of Carnegie Hall for the first time and said softly, "I think I'm gonna cry."

Ricky Skaggs, at the end of our Carnegie Hall concert, stood just off stage with only his mandolin, playing and singing "Rank Stranger" with Alison Krauss. Charley Pride later walked up and led them both in singing the old gospel favorite, "Mansions For Me." I stood nearby nursing a big-time case of goosebumps!

I told Gretchen Wilson that her recording, "I Don't Feel Like Loving You Today," is my favorite song on the radio these days. She replied with a grin, "Mine, too!"

Brad Paisley told me, "I never cry...but when you guys won that award, I actually had tears in my eyes. I was happier for you than I would have been had I won an award myself."

Vince Gill, backstage at Carnegie Hall, urged other entertainers to pick up the pace of the show because "the batteries in Whisper's yellow coat will run down in ten minutes."

Without a country radio station and limited exposure to our music via television, the New York natives aren't overly familiar with many of our country performers. Example: Brad Paisley and I had slipped into Alan Jackson's and Charley Pride's assigned dressing room backstage to rehearse our upcoming song when a young Carnegie Hall production assistant opened the door, looked first at one of us and then the other, and asked, "Mr. Pride?"

Opry announcer, Eddie Stubbs, told me of his first trip to Carnegie Hall as the fiddle player with The Johnson Mountain Boys bluegrass band. "I got a standing ovation on the most famous stage in the world on Saturday night. Monday morning I was back hanging wallpaper on my day job in D.C. That'll keep you humble!"

The warmth and friendliness shown to all us Tennessee hillbillies by the people of New York was remarkable. I hadn't been to the Big Apple in almost ten years, and the change in attitude that I had heard and read so much about is evident everywhere. It is definitely the new and improved New York City. I would not have been surprised to hear someone say, "Y'all come back now, you hear?"

Come to think of it, I probably will.

December 12, 2005

Hi Gang:

Well, I'm sure most of you are as busy as I am these days with all the last-minute preparations for the holidays, so I won't keep you.

But I did want to drop by for a minute to just say "thanks" to all our web site visitors, and to wish each of you a very Merry Christmas.

Notice I did not say "Happy Holidays" or offer some other generic greeting, but rather I said, "Merry Christmas." This is certainly not intended to offend anyone who worships in a faith other than Christianity, but I am a Christian, and at my house we wish one another a "Merry Christmas."

Regardless of your beliefs or mine, we need to wish one another love and peace and togetherness at this most special time of year. May our collective faiths serve to bind us closer to one another rather than to drive us farther apart.

Most of all, enjoy the season, and I hope you are blessed with the opportunity to share it with the ones you love the most.

December 26, 2005

Hi Gang:

I greet you on the day after the big day, hoping each of you had a wonderful Christmas and that you were able to spend it with the ones that you love. I went to Georgia and gained about twenty pounds at my sister Mary's house. She may have been battling cancer for almost three years, but it sure hasn't hurt her ability to cook and spread it out across her dining room table for all to enjoy.

For more years than I can remember, she has prepared a huge Christmas morning brunch and invited friends and strangers alike (my dad once referred to her guests as the "widows and orphans club") to join her and

her family in eating, opening gifts, eating, listening to Christmas songs, eating, visiting by the fire, and eating some more. After the last person has waddled out the door somewhere around two o'clock, she takes a quick nap then gets up and starts preparing (or as we say in the south "fixing") dinner. This time instead of quiche and sausage balls and fresh fruit and pastries, it's the traditional turkey and dressing with all the trimmings. I know it's not cool these days to say you like fruit cake, but you've never eaten fruit cake until you've had one made from my mama's recipe. Mary has preserved that wonderful recipe, and in her hands the dark, rich concoction still tastes like it did when I loved it so much as a young boy. Add a scoop of egg nog ice cream, and I double-dog dare you to leave more than a few crumbs scattered across your plate!
It was quite a Christmas. Now if you'll excuse me, I think I hear the treadmill calling my name.
Happy New Year!

Bill and His sister Mary

2006

January 2, 2006

Hi Gang:
Scroll down a bit.

See that empty space? That's the clean slate we are all starting off with here in the New Year. Notice there are no mistakes written there, no hurt feelings, no resentments. There's also no joy, no happiness, no excitement. There's nothing there. YET!
What we write upon the blank sheet of paper we've been given here at the beginning of 2006 is largely up to each one of us. What will fill that space 365-days from now? Regrets? Smiles? Conflicts? Peace? Would we really want to know now even if we could?
I can't imagine a much better year than I had in 2005. I'll certainly not win another "Song Of The Year" award this go-'round, but, Lord willing, in July I will get to celebrate my 45th anniversary as a member of the Grand Ole Opry. I plan to write some new songs, make some new recordings, hopefully make some new friends and bury some old hatchets this year. I hope I can keep on putting one foot in front of the other to the point where at the beginning of 2007 I can look back over my shoulder and say, "Wow, that was a GOOD ride!"
I wish nothing less for each of you.
Happy New Year!

January 9, 2006

Hi Gang:

The hook line to the title song in my latest album says, "Nobody asked me…that's just the way I feel."With that in mind, allow me to share a few of my recent personal observations:

When the temperature dips close to thirty-degrees Fahrenheit in Florida, it's colder than thirty-something degrees anywhere else on the planet! I guess it's the result of the constant wind blowing in off the nearby water. For that reason, the seven-thousand or so brave souls who bundled up and came our recent outdoor show at Cypress Gardens have my utmost respect and appreciation. I learned during our autograph session afterward that most of them were from up north, and had come to Florida to escape the cold weather back home!

The movie, "Walk The Line," based on Johnny Cash's life is much better than I had anticipated. Joaquin Phoenix doesn't really look or sound all that much like Johnny, but he plays the role in such a way that he's totally believable. Reese Witherspoon's portrayal of June Carter Cash, on the other hand, struck me as one-dimensional. Blame it on the script-writing if you will, but to me June was a much deeper, more complex person than the image we saw on the screen. I can see why Johnny's daughters were not pleased with the way their mother was depicted in the film. Vivian was much more attractive than the actress who played her part, and when we lived in California for a brief time in the early sixties, my wife and I found Vivian to be a warm and giving person. She was not pictured as such in the movie. I do hope the film wins some major awards though. Maybe it will inspire Hollywood to look even deeper inside the world of country music. Following our show in Florida, George "Goober" Lindsey and I had dinner at a very nice, upscale restaurant, and George ordered bananas foster for dessert. "It's my treat," he said. "I sold four pictures after the show!" The waiter, dressed in his crisp, black tuxedo, prepared the delicacy tableside with all the pomp and circumstance you might expect, then proudly placed the warm bananas, ice cream, and waffle-cone shell on the table. George looked up and, doing his best Goober impersonation, asked seriously, "You got any grape jam?" He is without a doubt one of the most naturally funny people I have ever been around.

But like I say, "Nobody asked me...that's just the way I feel."

January 17, 2006

Hi Gang:

And thanks for stopping by our web site.

If you're new to this particular spot on the internet, we welcome you. I hope you'll enjoy your visit, and check back in with us soon and often. For our regulars, you know that I usually try to share a few thoughts with you in this space every week or so. And I look forward to, and appreciate very much, your feedback. Sometimes you agree with what I say and other times you take issue, and either way is fine. I enjoy hearing from you, and try to respond whenever I can.

I don't normally make New Year's resolutions, but this year I have resolved to take a little more time off from my hectic lifestyle and smell a few of the roses I have bypassed over the years. I say that so you'll know when I don't have a new Whisper Column every Monday it's nothing personal. I'm not retiring, so please don't get that rumor started. I'm still going to write some new songs, appear on the Grand Ole Opry, host my XM radio show, record a new album, and tour whenever I can. But I'm going to try and do it at a more manageable pace than perhaps I have in the past. My younger daughter, her husband, and four of my grandchildren will be moving back to Nashville this summer, and I hope to spend more time with them…especially the one who wants to be a singer/dancer/musician and the one who wants to be an actress. ("Having you for a grandfather is really going to help!" my little nine- year old "actress" told me at Christmas!)

I'm probably going to watch a few more ball games, stare at a few more sunrises and sunsets, hike a few more mountain trails, and skip rocks across a few more rivers and streams than I have in recent years. I might even find time to finish the novel and the updated autobiography I began writing a hundred years or so ago.

I just wanted you to know. Wish me luck!

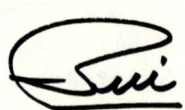

February 2, 2006

Hi Gang:

Several of you have contacted my office recently and said you are having trouble getting your e-mails to go through to me at billa@billanderson.com.

I'm sorry if you've had mail returned to you. Please know we are looking into the problem and, hopefully, we'll have it fixed soon.

Meantime, I'm beginning to feel like an expectant mother. No, my belly is not swollen (any more than usual!), and I'm not craving chocolate-covered pickles in the middle of the night, but I am involved in the last-minute labor pains from a couple of projects that are due to be "born" next month.

One is an in-store version of our "Live" DVD which, up until now, has only been available through our web site. It is being repackaged by Varese-Sarabande Records out in California, and the one-hour version, complete with new liner notes and photographs, will be available in record stores and video stores nationwide March 14th. .

My other new baby, due on the same exact date, will be a 20-song CD that MCA Records is releasing as part of their series, "The Definitive Collection." The interesting part about this package is that it contains many old photographs that most of you have probably never seen, and traces my career musically from 1960 through 1979. I'm particularly excited about the fact that the booklet will contain the original record number of every song, when each particular song was in the charts, how high it went in those charts, who produced each song, and a world of other information that has never been available on one of my CD's up to now. For example, in proofreading the copy while I was on a short vacation these past few days, I found that out of the twenty songs included, seven of them reached the #2 position in the charts!

People always talk about how many #1 records an artist has, but nobody ever mentions those that reached #2. I guess I'm like the car rental company that said for years they were #2 so they'd have to try harder! Maybe I should name one of my new babies Avis!

February 10, 2006

Hi Gang:

Well, we seem to have the e-mail problem fixed here at our web site, and the mail you send to us appears to be flowing again. Cross your fingers and let's hope it stays that way.

I guess I must have had "gremlins" in my computer. And some " gremlins" in my television cable box as well.

I have recently remodeled my in-home theater system, and I invited a group of my friends over to watch the Super Bowl. I was proud of my new big-screen, high-definition system with its surround-sound, and everybody was bragging on how clear the picture was and how great everything sounded…until the first play of the fourth quarter of the football game.

Whammo!! The "gremlins" struck again. This time they knocked out my picture, my sound, my entire system. So what did I do with a house full of guests who had come to watch the ball game in wide-screen, high definition? I did what any quick-thinking, red-blooded American football fan would do. I ran to my office and hauled out my six-inch black-and-white plastic TV with the rabbit-ears antenna!

(The younger ones among you are saying, "What are rabbit ears?" Go ask your grandparents. I don't have time to go into that right now!)

I just wish you could have seen my entire group of guests now STAND-ING in my kitchen and SQUINTING at this postage-stamp sized, snow-filled TV screen. Nobody said a word. We stood like robots until suddenly I looked around the room and broke out laughing. It was one of the funniest sights I have ever seen.

One of my guests said, "Well, you took us from the penthouse to the outhouse in one afternoon!" I made a mental note to not invite that person back for all the fun next year!

February 20, 2006

Hi Gang:

I was meeting with an attorney in another city a few days ago, when I realized I needed copies of some of the material he and I were going over. While he was shuffling papers, I left his office and went in search of a copy machine.

I found one just as a gray-haired, grandmotherly lady was finishing making some copies of her own. Being unfamiliar with the particular piece of equipment she had been using, I asked her if she'd mind making a couple of copies for me before she left the room.

She looked at me, smiled a beautiful smile, and said she'd be glad to. Then she added, "You've been here a long time, haven't you?" I looked at my watch and said it had only been a couple of hours.

"Oh, no," she said, "I mean you've been in the real estate business in this town for a long time." "I'm not in the real estate business," I answered. With a puzzled look on her face she asked, "You're not? Well, what do you do?" "I'm a country music singer," I replied.

She stared at me with a blank expression on her face. "What's your name?" she inquired. I answered that I was Bill Anderson.

"Of course!" she exclaimed. "I knew I had seen you somewhere. You're the one they call The Streaker, aren't you?"

"No, m'am," I said, trying hard to keep from laughing and embarrassing her. "That was Ray Stevens." She turned back to the copy machine, made my copies and handed them to me. All of a sudden a light seemed to go on in her mind. "NO," she squealed. "They call you The Whisperer!" I nodded, and she seemed delighted to have finally put the pieces of the puzzle together. I went back into the lawyer's office and we finished our business. As I was exiting the building, I saw my new friend huddled in the corner of the lobby with several other employees of the firm. She pointed toward me as I left, and I overheard her say to the others, "That's The Whisperer. I knew it was him the minute he walked in here. I'd have recognized that voice anywhere!"

I just smiled and streaked on out the door.

March 16, 2006

Hi Gang:

Have you had a chance to look over the list of nominees for the Academy of Country Music Awards coming up later this spring?

And I don't mean just the Keith Urbans, Brad Paisleys, Gretchen Wilsons and Rascal Flatts of our world. Those are folks whose names you'd expect to see at the top of anybody's list of country music favorites these days.

But dig a little deeper, scroll down a little farther, and you'll see that the Academy honors not only these deserving folks, but they also honor the musicians and other "background people" who stand outside the spotlight yet contribute so much to our genre of music.

I was particularly thrilled this year to look under the list of five nominees for Steel Guitar Player of the Year and see the names of two of my former band members, Sonny Garrish and Mike Johnson.

I brought Sonny to town when he was still in his late teens, and he responded by creating those incredible steel guitar licks on hits like "I Get The Fever", "Wild Weekend", and virtually everything else I recorded from 1966 to 1975. He was ultimately so successful that I had to wish him well and let him go. He's gone on to become one of Nashville's most outstanding session players, playing on hit record after hit record behind almost every big-name artist you can think of.

Mike Johnson had already played steel for Mel Street and Jack Greene before he came to work with me in the early eighties, but in the sixteen years that he was my steel player and band leader, he grew into one of the most dedicated and creative players I have ever known. Again, his success enabled him to get off a tour bus and into the recording studio on a full-time basis, the ultimate goal of most road musicians. Slowly but surely Mike has worked his way into the inner circle of session players, and today you'll see his name listed on the credits of many hit records coming out of Nashville.

The musicians who travel with the artists mile after mile, year after year, and then sit and stand behind us on stage day after day, night after night, are the true blue-collar, working-man heroes of our business. I formed my first Nashville band in 1964, and I can truly say that for over forty years I've had some of the very best and brightest working with me. I am exceptionally proud of Sonny and Mike right at this moment, though, and just wish there were some way they could each win the ACM award. I'm trying to figure out a way to sneak an extra ballot so I can vote for them both.

Mike Johnson

Sonny Garrish

March 27, 2006

Hi Gang:
Well, hillbilly heaven got a little more crowded and our earthly country music family grew significantly smaller this past week with the passing of two icons, songwriter Cindy Walker and the multi-talented Buck Owens. Both are members of the Country Music Hall of Fame.
From the time I was old enough to read and study the song lyrics on the pages of Country Song Roundup magazine, I was aware of Cindy Walker. Her name seemed to always be attached to several of each month's top songs, everything from the plaintive "Bubbles In My Beer" to the poignant "You Don't Know Me." Harlan Howard once referred to Cindy as "the teacher," and he was right. We all learned from her masterful crafting of words and melodies, and hopefully we learned a little from

her unaffected charm and grace as well. She was a marvelous lady.
Few people have ever mentioned Buck Owens and Bill Anderson in the
same sentence, but, looking back, he and I walked strangely parallel
paths in many ways. We were both radio disc jockeys in the late fifties
and experienced our first musical success in the early sixties. We each
wrote most of our own recorded material and each surrounded ourselves
with outstanding bands of musicians. We both ended up owning radio
stations and being about as well known for our work in television as for
our work in music. Ironic that we shared a CMA Award together in 2001,
along with Brad Paisley and George Jones, for our joint recording of
"Too Country." Aside from his incredible singing style and his trademark
Telecaster guitar picking, Buck was a savvy businessman who had both
the vision and the fortitude to stand up to his record company years ago
and strike a deal whereby he eventually would own his own master
recordings. That's not so out of the ordinary today, but back in his time,
it spoke volumes about his street-smarts and his stature as an artist.
Buck was known for his trademark red, white, and blue guitars, and he
often had replicas made and presented them to his friends. I have one
with an engraved inscription that refers to me as a "gentleman"
and a "friend."

Same to you, pal. We're gonna miss you.

Brad Paisley, Bill, Buck Owens and George Jones

April 6, 2006

Hi Gang:

Well, you've probably noticed we have a new item for sale inside our little "Whisper Store," and it's something that we are extremely excited about. My fan club president, Jean Brown, has spent the better part of this past year collecting recipes from country music stars, their wives and families, and country music fans from all around the country. She has now put them all together inside incredible new cookbook called, "Award Winning Whispers From The Kitchen," and we're making it available to cooks and chefs everywhere for the very first time.

Some of the recipes are ones that my mother prepared for our family during my growing-up (and growing-out!) years and later passed down to my sister. Others are from folks like Jim Ed Brown, who tells us how to make Party Punch and Roasted Pheasant. Joe Diffie chimes in with Cranberry Salad, Jeanne Seely gives us the instructions as to how to prepare a Pork Chop Dinner, and Steve Wariner shares his recipe for Crumbly Apple Pie. Jan Howard even reveals the secret ingredients in Jan's Strawberry Cake.

And for the folks who like good ole Cajun cooking from down in the bayou country of Louisiana, the Alligator Man himself, Jimmy C. Newman (along with more than a little help from his wife, Miss Mae), offers up a Cajun Chicken Sauce Picante. I'm getting hungry just writing about it!!

All the members of my Po' Folks Band contributed recipes as well, including piano player Ziggy Johnson's very own personal recipe for "Toast." You've got to see that one to believe it!

Plus, our fan club members from every corner of the USA chimed in with their own recipes, giving readers new ideas for outstanding dishes from all regions and cultures.

We are finding that many of our members are buying one cookbook for themselves and then ordering others as gifts. With Mother's Day right around the corner, you might want to consider one of these hard-cover, brightly illustrated books for that special Mom in your life.

If you like to eat (and you can tell by my waistline that I certainly do!) then this collection of outstanding recipes is for you. There's even a "Recipe To Live By." That's one we all need to follow.

122

You can click on our Merch section and order directly from the web site if you'd like.
Thanks, and we'll see you at the dinner table!

AWARD WINNING WHISPERS
FROM THE KITCHEN

WHISPERING BILL ANDERSON
INTERNATIONAL FAN CLUB

April 17, 2006

Hi Gang:

The "Grand Ole Opry At Carnegie Hall" DVD went on sale to the public last Tuesday, and I was invited to appear inside the Grand Ole Opry store and autograph first-day copies for an hour prior to our Tuesday night show.

I was having a lot of fun signing my name, posing for pictures, and meeting folks from all over the country when one lady handed me her DVD and asked, "Was this the first time you had ever performed in New York City?"

I smiled and told her, no, that I had performed there many times. And my mind went racing back across the years.

The first time I could recall doing a show in the greater New York area was in the very early sixties when Skeeter Davis and I were booked into an ethnic meeting hall in Brooklyn. There was virtually no country music on the radio in the city back then, and nobody at the hall (including the band they had hired to back us up) had ever heard of Skeeter Davis OR Bill Anderson.

I made many pilgrimages back to New York in subsequent years. I appeared on the game show, "To Tell The Truth," when I was so well unknown that two of the four panelists on the show guessed that a bookstore clerk from Birmingham was "the real Bill Anderson." I performed with an all-star cast of country artists at the old Madison Square Garden in 1964, worked for a week on several different occasions inside the Nashville Room at the Taft Hotel later that decade, and spent a lot of time in the late seventies and early eighties playing the demanding role of country singer, Bill Anderson, on the ABC-TV soap opera, "One Life To Live."

But the one New York moment I will never forget, in addition to last November's incredible evening at Carnegie Hall, was the time very early in my career when Jan Howard and I were booked into a small nightclub there on a cold November night. We had been warned that this particular venue did not have much in the way of dressing rooms, so we each decided to put on our stage wear at the hotel and wear long overcoats en route. The only part of my costume that was visible as we climbed into a taxi was my trademark white western boots.

124

We rode along in silence for a moment when the driver couldn't hold it in any longer. He looked at me through his rearview mirror and said, "You're a country music star, aren't you?"

Wow, I thought to myself. I must really be doing well for a cab driver in New York City to recognize me! I gave him my best aw-shucks grin and confessed that, yes, I was in the country music business. My mistake was in asking him, "How did you know?"

"Because," he replied, "I saw the white boots. And I knew nobody would wear white boots in New York City in November except a country music star or a damned fool!"

At least he gave me the benefit of the doubt.

April 27, 2006

Hi Folks:

And welcome to our web site. Thanks so much for stopping by.
We get first-time visitors nearly every day, and we appreciate you more
than you know. I hope you'll check out our News page for all the latest
happenings, our Tour page for our upcoming concert dates and
appearances at the Grand Ole Opry, as well as our Music and
Merchandise pages for the latest in the recordings, videos, and
souvenir items we offer for sale.

The cookbook is our newest project, and from what I hear, it's full of
incredible recipes. Here's a thought: Order a cookbook, create a
wonderful meal, and invite me over. I'm not much of a cook myself,
but I can eat with the best of them!

You can always write us directly at one of the two addresses listed
below. I enjoy hearing from you and answer as much of your e-mail as
possible. Hopefully, I'll be seeing you somewhere soon along the concert
trail, at the Grand Ole Opry, or over the airwaves on XM Satellite radio.
Thanks again for visiting our site, and my best wishes to you all.

May 24, 2006

Hi Folks:

And thanks for stopping by our web site today.

I was just checking my calendar and realized that our 10th annual City Lights Festival in my adopted hometown of Commerce, Georgia, is less than a month away. If you haven't already made your plans to come be with us, I hope you'll be making them soon.

Singer Mark Wills, along with the Funniest Man In America, comedian James Gregory, will be providing top-notch entertainment at our Dinner With the Stars on Thursday night June 22nd, while George Hamilton IV, the International Ambassador of Country Music, joins us for our first-ever Luncheon With the Stars on Friday June 23rd. It's your chance to hear, see, and visit with these folks up close and personal…an opportunity you may never have again. Besides, we'll feed you some of the best country cookin' you ever sank your teeth into! You can scroll down this page and click onto the City Lights icon for more details. I was also remembering today that Billy Walker donated his time to help provide the entertainment at our very first Dinner With the Stars some seven years ago. As always, he was the consummate performer and perfect gentleman. Our dinner that year was held at the First Methodist Church in Commerce, and I recall Billy not only singing in his warm, unmistakable style, but taking a moment or two to share his Christian faith with those in attendance as well. His death over the weekend leaves a large void within our Grand Ole Opry family and within our music industry as a whole. He was one of the first nationally known recording stars I ever met, and the very first one I ever introduced on stage. I was fortunate to have known him for almost fifty-years. He will be missed by friends and fans everywhere.

Billy Walker

June 8, 2006

Hi Gang:
Well, once again it's that crazy week here in Nashville known as the CMA Music Festival…or, to us ole dogs who have trouble learning new tricks, it's Fan Fair time!

Country music fans are here from all over the world for a week of concerts, autographs, photographs, picnics, parties, and parades. We welcome those of you who made the annual pilgrimage to Music City, and for those of you at home, here's hoping you can be with us sometime in the near future.

I was in my fan club booth for two hours earlier today greeting old friends and hopefully making some new ones. My favorite booth visitor was a little curly-headed, five-year old boy who handed me a guitar pick with his name on it. I asked him, "Are you going to be a guitar player when you grow up?" He thought for a minute and gave me a great answer. "Well," he said, "I want to either be a guitar player, a tattoo artist, or an astronaut!" Now there's a combination!

I have been to every single Fan Fair but one since its inception in 1972. I missed the event in 1985 only because I was in the hospital. I was told last week by a well-respected journalist in our city, Peter Cooper, that I've probably signed more autographs here than any other artist.

I've enjoyed every minute of it, too. I guess the only downside might be that if there's that many autographs of mine floating around out there, they'll probably never be worth very much on e-Bay!!

Have fun, and y'all come!

Roger Miller once said about his wife: "Her cooking is so bad all the flies in the neighborhood got together and fixed our screen door."

128

June 12, 2006

Hi Gang:

Well, the event formerly known as Fan Fair was a big success and a lot of fun. Thanks to all of you who stopped by our fan club booth for a visit. I enjoyed meeting each of you, and hope we can do it again real soon.

But for now, it's back to life in the real world.

I need to mention that our scheduled concert in Bethlehem, Pennsylvania, this coming Sunday, June 18th, has been canceled, or at least postponed until later in the year. I always hate it when things like this happen, but sometimes they can't be avoided. Keep watching our Tour page for further information.

Everything is still on track for the big 10th annual City Lights Festival in Commerce, Georgia, next week, though, and if you haven't made your plans to come be with us, I hope you'll do so soon. June 22nd is our big Dinner With The Stars where you'll get fed a wonderful, home-cooked southern meal and be entertained by singer Mark Wills and comedian James Gregory. The following day at noon, it's our first-ever Luncheon With The Stars featuring another delicious meal and the songs and stylings of George Hamilton IV. You can phone 877-XXX-XXXX for more details.

Thanks for visiting our web site, and thanks for all the nice e-mails you continue to send my way. I can't always reply to them all, but I read each and every one and always appreciate hearing from you.

Stay cool.

Veteran Opry musician, Charlie Collins, was once performing at the Opryland Park and had four of his tapes for sale after the show.

"Which one of those tapes has the most fiddle music on it?" a potential customer asked. Charlie pointed to a particular tape and smiled proudly, "This one."

The customer said, "Well give me the other three. I hate fiddle music."

June 19, 2006

I wish every person who reads this could have known my sister.
Mary was part Florence Nightingale and part Milton Berle. An old hippie and the consummate diva. A burgundy pillow with gold embroidery rested atop her bed. It read, "The queen will not be taking an audience today."
When she was only fourteen-years old and training to hopefully someday become an Olympic swimmer, she contracted lupus and was told she probably would not live to adulthood. If she did, she was warned she could never have children. But Mary was too headstrong to accept that diagnosis. She died last week at age 64 with two wonderfully healthy sons.
She could be the kindest, gentlest, most compassionate person you might have ever imagined, a rehabilitation nurse who worked primarily with brain-injured patients and their families. She encouraged them, giving them reasons to dream and hopes for a better tomorrow. And then, perhaps as a way to put aside the towering pressures of her job, she could turn into the wittiest, funniest, most off-the-wall person I've ever known.

I'm sure in her previous life she was a court-jester. I always told her she should have been the writer and performer in the family, not me.
She loved flowers. Oh, how she loved flowers. A few weeks before her death she told me, "When they write my obituary, make sure they put 'in lieu of flowers, please send flowers'!" And folks did. I never saw quite as many beautiful flower arrangements as adorned the little chapel where we celebrated her life and mourned our loss last Friday.
For each of you who sent flowers or an e-mail, a card, or a letter…for each of you who sent prayers upstairs on behalf of me and my family…thank you from the bottom of my heart. I wish I could thank you individually, but the sheer numbers make that impossible.

Mary fought a four-and-a-half year battle with ovarian cancer. It finally took her body, but it never took her mind, and it knew better than to try and mess with her spirit. Her old heart finally stopped beating, but her new one has started. Trust me, Heaven will never be the same!
I take great comfort in the words of the old song: "Farther along we'll know

all about it. Farther along we'll understand why."
But for now, I can only say "thank you" again, and may God bless you all.

June 26, 2006

Hi Gang:

When I was a kid, there was nothing I loved more than going to Lakewood Park in Atlanta and riding an old wooden roller coaster called the Greyhound.

It wasn't one of the fancy steel, hang-by-your-nails, flip-you-upside-down type roller coasters that fill amusement parks today, but the steep inclines followed by the seemingly bottomless drops, twists, and turns on that rickety old structure offered thrills-a-plenty for me. It cost twenty-five cents to ride, and I would save my allowance for weeks just to be able to hand the attendant another quarter every time the car pulled into the station so that I could go around again.

At the time, I thought I was simply riding a roller coaster. Little did I realize those rides were preparing me for this thing called "life."

Just a few days ago, following the death of my sister, I felt as though I was at the absolute bottom of the steepest incline in the world. I had stood in the little Georgia cemetery and seen all the members of my original family lying side by side…my mother, who died in 2001…my dad who died in 2003…and now my only sibling. In less than five years I had lost them all. I had never felt quite so alone.

But I noticed the roller coaster begin slowly climb the hill again after I came home to hundreds upon hundreds of e-mails, sympathy cards, letters, and telephone messages of condolence and assurance. People cared and they let me know it, and I felt their love all around me. It helped tremendously, but I still had to force myself to go back to work. The first day back, though, I learned for certain that a song I co-wrote, "I'll Wait For You," is going to be Joe Nichols' next single record. Joe has had two big hits in a row, and the record company thinks this could well be the biggest of them all. They plan to release it in late July or early August, complete with a major-production video. The car had begun its slow but steady climb back toward the top of the roller coaster for sure. And then, only a few hours later, I found out that another song that I helped to write is George Strait's new single. It's called "Give It Away," and it's already on the air or on its way to a radio station near you. Add to that our 10th annual successful City Lights Festival in Commerce, Georgia…large, enthusiastic, and responsive crowds at our weekend concerts in Wisconsin and Minnesota…and in less time than it takes to tell it, my personal roller coaster has somehow managed to creep its way back up toward the top of its highest peak.

Like any good roller coaster, though, there will be other corners and curves up ahead and at some point in the future I know things will level off and eventually even descend again. I understand that now, and I can accept it as part of life's overall plan.

But right this minute…thanks to many of you…the view from back up here near the top is pretty doggoned incredible!!

July 5, 2006

Hi Gang:

I had quite a surprise awaiting me when I arrived for our tenth annual City Lights Festival in my adopted hometown of Commerce, Georgia, back in late June.

I knew my invited guests, Mark Wills, James Gregory, and George Hamilton IV, would all be there and would delight the crowds, and they were and they did. But I had no idea that the members of the very first band I formed when I was in the tenth grade in high school would show up as well. But they did

I went to Avondale High School outside Atlanta, and my first band was known as the Avondale Playboys. It's hard to believe it now, but we were billed as "Georgia's Youngest Hillbilly Band."

It had been over fifty years since I had seen some of them. But all the ones in this picture were there: Jerry Jones, me, and Charles Wynn from the front row and Billy Moore and Jimmy "Meatball" Bell from the back. Two others who joined the band at various times, Bobby Snipes and Lamar Worthy, were there as well. None of them have continued with music other than as a hobby. When I asked them if they would like to play a song, Lamar said, "Sure, as long as it's in G. I never learned to play in any other key!" I can't tell you what a thrill it was to have them there. We laughed, told old war stories about the nights when we would play for tips, the days when we got fired from radio and television stations (once because Meatball told the manager of a radio station that he had a light bulb at home more powerful than the station...and once because our loud rehearsals drowned out the six o'clock news on TV!), and all the fun we had in between. I find it amazing that we're all still alive and in reasonably good health all these years later. Nothing in life is more important than strong, lasting friendships. And nothing is more precious than warm, happy memories. Thanks to these guys, my cup today is overflowing with both.

Front Row: Jerry Jones, Bill, Charles Wynn
Back Row: Billy Moore, Jimmy Bell

July 17, 2006

Hi Gang:

I've been singing about wild weekends ever since I wrote and recorded a song by that name back in the late sixties.

But I'm here to tell you, I just experienced one first-hand!

As you may know, July 15th marked my 45th Anniversary as a member of the Grand Ole Opry. Over three-hundred members of my fan club signed up to come to Nashville and help me celebrate. And celebrate we did!

It would take more space than I've got here to relate to you all the activities we found ourselves caught up in, but they included radio shows, television shows, private dinners and concerts, question and answer sessions, meet 'n greet autograph and photo parties, and just about everything else you can imagine….except sleep!

We'll have some pictures up on the web site shortly and Country Weekly magazine, I'm told, will be doing a story on the festivities. Meantime, I want to thank all the fan club members who came (I've often said that I don't have the most fans in country music, but I've sure got the best!), my fan club president, Jean Brown, who put so many hours into planning and coordinating the events, and the hundreds of you who sent cards, letters, and e-mails of congratulations. The calendar says it's been 45-years, but honestly, it seems like only yesterday.

The past six weeks of my life have included taking part in the 2006 version of Fan Fair, our 10th annual City Lights Festival in Commerce, and now the 45th Anniversary celebration at the Opry. Sandwiched in between was the emotionally draining death of my sister. As you might imagine, I'm in serious need of a little rest and relaxation, so I'm disappearing for a couple of weeks' worth of vacation.

People are always telling me to slow down and take time to smell the roses, so here I go.

Thanks for everything, and I'll see you when I get back.

July 31, 2006

Hi Gang:

For some reason, I've often had trouble over the years truly enjoying my vacations.

I spent some time on my most recent one trying to figure out why.

I've come to the conclusion that the human body, much like an automobile, a motorcycle, or a speedboat, is not built to go immediately from one-hundred miles an hour to a complete standstill. In the past, I think I've tried to bypass the downshifting process and just slammed on the brakes.

Guess what? It doesn't work.

This year I marked off enough time to slowly ease my way from 78 rpm down to 45 rpm and eventually down to 33 1/3 rpm before I stopped completely. (Some of you older folks may have to explain that to this younger generation of iPod and MP3 users!) I tend to forget how hard I press the pedal to the metal most of the time. Between songwriting, recording, touring, working the Opry, taping my radio show, and the million and one other things I find myself unable to say "no" to, it's pretty much open-throttle for me twenty-four/seven.

But I managed to shut 'er down gradually over the past two weeks, and it was wonderful. I said I was going to "smell the roses", and I did. I also smelled some tall, green pine trees, some lobster cooking over an open flame, and the salt air easing its way in over a sandy beach. I climbed some mountain trails, meandered down some city streets, ate some delicious food, plodded my way around a golf course (and remembered why I gave up the game years ago), and got a whole lot of much-needed rest and sleep.

I came away from it all with a couple of observations. First, once you get north of, say, Boston, the people of Vermont, New Hampshire, and Maine are almost like southerners. They can't seem to cover you with enough down-home hospitality. And second, contrary to popular belief, there is a lot of country music in New England!

At one point, I had each of the six pre-set buttons on my rental car radio locked into a different country station, with at least two more signals trying valiantly to worm their way in through the static. I heard advertisements for several upcoming concerts featuring "Massachusetts' own" Jo

Dee Messina, Tracy Lawrence, Rodney Atkins, the Grascals, and Blue County. I was tuned in when a young lady phoned a noontime request show and asked for, "..that new one, 'Give It Away', by George Strait. It's an awesome song!" she exclaimed. I couldn't help but wonder what her reaction would have been had she known one of the song's co-writers was listening.

The weather wasn't perfect (but whose was?) and the Braves' winning streak came to an end while I was gone, but I'm back home, refreshed, and ready to go back to work. At least for a week or so.

By then I'll be ready for another vacation!

August 14, 2006

Hi Gang:

Thanks for stopping by our web site today. I hope you will enjoy your visit.

I guess most of you have seen in the news over this past weekend where longtime afternoon television host, Mike Douglas, passed away. He died on his 81st birthday.

They have shown clips over the past few days of a three-year old Tiger Woods hitting a golf ball on Mike's show, and of newlywed Tiny Tim showing off his baby daughter from the same venue. You may have read where Mike hosted over 30,000 guests in the 21-years his show was syndicated across America from 1961 to 1982.

But nowhere did you read, nor will you, who the first country music artist was to appear on the Mike Douglas Show. But it happened to be yours truly.

His show was only seen on a handful of stations when I was invited in for my initial guest appearance in what must have been 1963. The show was taped in Cleveland in those days, prior to Mike's career-expanding move to Philadelphia. I didn't even have a full band of my own back then, but walked into his studio with the two musicians I did employ, steel guitar great, Weldon Myrick, and my lead guitar player, Jimmy Lance.

At that time, Mike, who was a big-band, pop-styled singer himself, had a small three or four piece jazz-style combo that provided music for his show. When Weldon, Jimmy, and I walked into the studio to set up our country music instruments and rehearse for our segment, one of the staff musicians looked down from the bandstand and said disparagingly in a voice loud enough for us all to hear, "Well, THIS will set our show back ten years!"

Fortunately, it didn't. Mike was extremely gracious to us, and went on to invite us back on numerous occasions. There is a picture in my autobiography taken the day I visited his show with Carol Channing. Once I was his guest along with football icon, Don Meredith, who introduced Mike that afternoon to a "hot new singer from Texas" named Willie Nelson. Jimmy Dean recalls inviting Mel Tillis to the Mike Douglas show when the sausage king was Mike's co-host. Nobody on Mike's staff knew who Mel Tillis was until about two days prior to his arrival. "We can't have someone on the show who has a speech impediment," they gasped in horror. Jimmy simply told them to relax and let Mel do his thing which they did. Mel, of course, fractured the audience, leading to his and Jimmy's and countless other country music stars' being asked back time and time again.

I recall Mike Douglas coming to Nashville on several occasions, and my manager and I introduced him to down-home southern cooking at a restaurant several miles outside the city limits called the Loveless Café. He and his wife, Gen, fell in love with the southern fried chicken, country ham, and homemade biscuits and preserves. Every time he would return to Music City, even if I weren't there to drive him, he'd have to visit Loveless. The restaurant manager told me one time that Mike Douglas was the only person who ever pulled up in front of this small, non-descript country café in a black stretch limousine with a chauffeur!

The Mike Douglas Show was a kind and gentle show, because its host was a kind and gentle man. It was a far cry from the bug-swallowing reality shows and the screaming-fit Jerry Springer shows of today. But then, in those days, I guess we lived in a kinder, gentler time.

I don't know about you, but I miss that.

Mike Douglas, Mary Lou Turner
with Bill

Mike Douglas

September 6, 2006

Hi Gang:

I spent the Labor Day weekend on a boat called the Mississippi Queen cruising the Tennessee River, embarking and disembarking in Alabama. And you think your life is confusing!

It was my first actual cruise aboard a paddle-wheeling steamboat, even though early in my career I wrote a #1 song for Faron Young called "Riverboat." In the song, I told the story of a man who made his living as a professional card dealer aboard a boat traveling the Mississippi River from St. Paul to New Orleans. On one of the boat's southbound excursions, a high-roller accused the man of dealing from the bottom of the deck, a scuffle ensued, and the professional gambler shot and killed the passenger. The authorities came on board the riverboat when it docked in Memphis and took the dealer to jail, proving that crime doesn't pay. Or at least it didn't back in 1960.

Having composed that little piece of musical fiction, naturally the first thing I asked to see when we boarded the Mississippi Queen was the casino. I wanted to see if I had pictured it correctly in my mind all these years. Imagine my surprise when I found out that actual floating riverboats do not, in fact, even have casinos.

It has to do with various state laws, I'm told. Casinos are allowed on floating barges that are anchored to dry land, but not allowed upon boats that cross state lines. I'm not a movie buff, but I could have sworn I used to see gambling halls (or at least floating poker games) on board river-going vessels in the movies. But then those were only movies. And my story was only a song.

Anyhow, the riverboat cruise was nicer, more genteel, and overall a far better experience than I had envisioned. It's much more intimate than a large cruise ship, carrying 300-plus passengers as opposed to three-thousand. The décor was 1920's elegant and so realistic that I expected at any moment to look up and find myself face-to-face with Humphrey Bogart or at least Huckleberry Finn. The food was delicious…I ate far too much…and the friendly service was impeccable.

I was surprised in talking with other passengers to find that so many had come from the far west…California, Arizona, Washington, Oregon, and Wyoming…to sail the rivers of the southeast. "Your rivers here are so much more peaceful than ours," a lady from Portland, Oregon, told me. Most of the passengers seemed to be country music fans and were very generous with their applause for Little Jimmy Dickens and yours truly. Overall, it was an experience I would highly recommend, and one I would be more than willing to try again. But I do wish someone would tell me what they did with the casinos!!

Who driving this boat?

September 18, 2006

Hi Gang:

Trust me on this one:

There is no better way in the world to wake up than for your music publisher to call first thing in the morning and confirm that you have, indeed, co-written the current #1 song in all of country music!

That's how my day started today, and in spite of the rain falling from the skies, my world right now is nothing but sunshine!

The song, of course, is "Give It Away" by the amazingly talented George Strait. It's the first song of mine that George has ever recorded, and I'm told that with this #1 hit, George now holds the all-time record for #1 songs in country music. Along with my co-writers, Jamey Johnson and Buddy Cannon, we are proud and grateful to be a small part of such a monumental achievement. George, as you know, will be inducted into the Country Music Hall of Fame in November. And deservedly so.

Somebody has already asked me how many #1 songs this makes in my career, and I honestly do not know. I've been too busy trying to write them to stop and count. I even had one news reporter ask me if I ever get tired of having hit songs. I just stared at him and laughed until he realized the absurdity of his question.

Of course, none of this would ever happen without the fans, so to each of you, thanks for continuing to make this ole whisperin' hillbilly's dreams come true.

Life is good.

George Strait

October 02, 2006

Hi Gang:

I had the opportunity to attend a very unusual music business party last week.

BNA Records had an invitation-only gathering at the new Musicians Hall of Fame building in downtown Nashville to honor superstar Kenny Chesney on the occasion of his having sold 25,000,000 records over the course of his career.

I should have known the party was not going to be the typical sho-biz ego fest when I first walked in the door. The first person I bumped into was the last person I expected to see right away, the guest of honor himself. I had expected to stand in a long line of well-wishers in order to just offer my congratulations. Instead, there stood Kenny in a t-shirt, ball cap, and jeans having his picture made with George Jones. Never one to be camera shy, I slid in beside him and asked if he'd mind smiling for one more shot. He obliged, introduced me to his mother and his uncle, and went about his business of being, perhaps, the most humble honoree in the history of Music City.

We munched on some delicious bits of finger-food and listened as label head, Joe Galante, and others praised Kenny's success and presented him with a couple of obligatory plaques. Kenny shuffled to the stage and in his aw-shucks east Tennessee manner accepted the praise and adulation. And then the whole affair took a very unexpected 180-degree turn. They asked everyone in the crowded room to turn to their left and face a long wall draped in black. I assumed, along with almost everyone else in attendance, that the drape would be removed and some kind of life-sized statue or picture or plaque honoring Kenny would be revealed. Boy, were we all surprised.

The drape was dropped, all right, but instead of revealing something dedicated to Kenny and his remarkable achievement, there hung at least a couple hundred colorful, personally engraved plaques honoring the people in that room…the songwriters, the music publishers, the support personnel…all the people who had helped contribute in some way to Kenny's remarkable success.

"Nobody sells twenty-five million records without a lot of help," Kenny said, "and I just want y'all to know how much I appreciate what each one

142

of you has done." He then invited us all to approach the wall and remove our own individual plaques.

Kenny has been kind enough to record two-songs that I helped write, the hit, "A Lot Of Things Different," and an obscure novelty song from his album of island-themed material called "Key Lime Pie." As a result, there was a plaque there with my name on it. It now hangs proudly on my office wall.

Sometimes only the bad news makes it into print. The tabloids aren't interested in a warm, feel-good story like this, but I thought you should know. What Kenny Chesney did that afternoon was 100% pure class. Just like him.

Kenny Chesney and Bill

October 10, 2006

Hi Gang:

I went back to college this past weekend.

Well, I didn't actually go back to class, but I went down to the University of Georgia to see a football game for the first time since 1980. The trip brought back a lot of memories. The campus was just as alive and the coeds just as pretty as I remembered. Walking toward Sanford Stadium, I passed by the Fine Arts Auditorium where, as a student, I once entered a songwriting contest. There were only two contestants, me and one other guy. His song won. For years I told everybody I "came in second," which was the truth, but just barely. Once I reached my seat, I tried to see the dormitory room where I used to live, but it was hidden behind the two upper decks they have since added to the football stadium. When I was in school, I could stand at my window and watch games on the field below. I saw Fran Tarkenton, who went on to become a star at Georgia and a Hall of Fame professional quarterback, lead his high school team to the state championship from that very window. A big crowd for a college game in those days was 30,000 fans. Saturday's game drew over 92,000 and played to a nationwide television audience.

I once had the opportunity in the early seventies to perform during halftime of a Georgia game, singing from the field with my own Po' Boys band, augmented by the school's Dixie Redcoat Marching Band. What a thrill that was! It may have been the largest single crowd I ever performed for, although the stadium seated "only" 70,000 at that time.

I saw several longtime friends this weekend and one good ole boy dressed in a tight red t-shirt with a face to match. He sported an ample beer-belly that he was obviously attempting to expand. He approached me and said, "When you were in college, you couldn't sing worth a (bleep). You've sure come a long way!" I wondered who told him.

Unfortunately, during my college years, Georgia didn't win very many foot-ball games. They've done much better recently and were actually undefeated going into Saturday night's game against Tennessee. Somebody must have told them I was there, though, because they reverted to their old ways and snatched defeat from the jaws of victory. Late in the first half they were leading 24-7, but ended up losing 51-33.

Like I said, my visit brought back a lot of memories.

October 26, 2006

Hi Gang:

I got carded last night.

That's right, carded. C-A-R-D-E-D. Like when a young person goes into a convenience store and tries to buy a six-pack of beer and the person behind the counter says, "Let me see your driver's license." In effect what they are saying is, "I don't believe you are twenty-one and old enough to buy beer."

No, I wasn't trying to buy beer. I was trying to pay for my groceries. See, the supermarket where I shop has a senior citizen discount on Wednesdays. It's not much, something like 5%, but there were signs everywhere advertising the discount which is available only on Wednesdays. I hadn't gone to the store because it was Wednesday but rather because my refrigerator was empty. But I saw the sign, realized what day it was, and when the young lady rang up my total I said, "What about my discount?"

"Sir, that's only for people sixty years old," she replied.

"So?"

"You're not sixty years old!" she announced. Her companion who had been sacking my groceries nearby added, "Well if he is, he sure carries it well!" It was at that very moment I decided to remember both those young ladies in my will.

I flashed my driver's license with all the bravado of someone who had just celebrated his twenty-first birthday. "See," I said, "I qualify!" The cashier took 5% off my bill.

The girl at the end of the counter then offered to push my cart full of groceries to my car. "Hey," I exclaimed, "I may be old but I'm not feeble!" I pushed my own cart, thank you very much, and walked sprightly to my vehicle.

I was grinning all the way.

November 1, 2006

Hi Gang:

I couldn't have been more than 30-years old the afternoon my record producer, the legendary Owen Bradley, walked into the studio control room wearing an uncustomary coat and tie.

Without speaking a word, he slowly removed his coat and draped it across the back of his chair. He sat down and loosened his tie, exhaled and shook his head slowly. He looked up at me with resignation and said softly, "Bill, you'll know you're getting old someday when you go to more funerals than you do weddings."

I didn't understand the full meaning of his words back then. At thirty years of age, who thinks about things like getting old and dying? Today, though, I know what he meant full-well.

Within the past two weeks, four people who touched my life in the music business have passed away: Allen Whitcomb, a close friend and my former booking agent; Tillman Franks, who once booked me on the Louisiana Hayride long before I was ready for such a lofty appearance; Marijohn Wilkin, one of the finest songwriters ever to grace our business; and early today the man who probably had more to do with my becoming a professional songwriter and recording artist than any other single individual, Buddy Killen. Buddy succumbed to cancer in the wee hours of my birthday morning.

I could write volumes about Buddy Killen, but suffice it to say that he was the first music publisher in Nashville to ask the skinny kid from Georgia who had written "City Lights" if he might have any other songs tucked away somewhere. When I told him that I did, he asked to hear them. Through his publishing company, Tree International, he published every song I wrote for the next four years and for many years thereafter. He introduced me to Owen Bradley, helped me secure a three-year recording contract with Decca Records that lasted for twenty-three years, and even played bass behind me the first night I performed on the Grand Ole Opry.

He and I came up with the country-disco idea together and co-wrote both "I Can't Wait Any Longer," my last number one record, and the infamous, "Double S." We enjoyed a Jim Reeves hit with a song we co-wrote called, "Losing Your Love." Our biggest success as co-authors, however, came when Conway Twitty topped the charts in 1979 with a song we had written twenty years earlier, "I May Never Get To Heaven."

Buddy and I were more than business associates...we were friends. One of the most memorable New Years' Eves of my life was the one I spent a few years ago with Buddy and his wife, Carolyn, at their condo in Wyoming. Along with Donna and Jimmy Dean, we rode a horse-drawn sleigh up a snow-covered mountain to welcome the New Year over dinner and drinks inside a small, rustic cabin in front of a roaring fire.

We are told from the day we are born that death is a part of life, and surely it is. It will come to us all sooner or later, and there's nothing we can do about it. Buddy was a good man, and those of us left behind don't have to worry about his "not getting to heaven" as our song says. He's probably up there already trying to get Hank or Waylon or Johnny to record one of his songs.

Meantime, I wish somebody would invite me to a wedding.

Buddy Killen

November 10, 2006

Hi Gang:
I have had, as the kids would say, two "cool" things happen over the
past week, both of which involved e-mails sent to me at this web site
address. I thought you might enjoy reading about them.
First, I received an e-mail from a total stranger who works at a college in
Ohio. He asked if I had ever had a band called The Avondale Playboys,
and said that if I had, he had something I might be interested in.
I wrote back and told him, yes, when I was in high school down in
Georgia, that was the name of my first little hillbilly band.
He then wrote back and told me that he had somehow come across a
scratchy old 78rpm acetate recording of Bill Anderson & The Avondale
Playboys playing and singing a commercial jingle for a politician who
was running for Congress. The politician's name was James C. Davis.
Well, James C. Davis was a close friend of my father's, and in the far
recesses of my mind I seemed to recall writing and recording a song for
him when I was 15 or 16-years old. It was to the tune of "Y'all Come"
and was called, "Y'all Vote." (I didn't know back then that you couldn't
write new lyrics to someone else's melody without their permission. May
the late Arlie Duff forgive me!)
Making a long story as short as I can, this very nice man had access to
some modern-day recording equipment at his university, and has now e-
mailed me a digitally re-mastered copy of "Y'all Vote." He and his wife
are coming to Nashville soon and will bring me the original record, which
he says has a handwritten label on it. I can't wait to see if the handwrit-
ing is mine.
So, how cool is that?
And then, only a few days later, I received another e-mail from a lady in
Texas telling me that her mother, whom I have also never met, will be
coming to the Opry on November 21st and would like very much for me
to sing, "I Wonder If God Likes Country Music," the song I recorded
many years ago with Roy Acuff.
The writer went on to tell me that her mom's dream had always been to
see and hear me perform that song live on stage. The reason? Because
her mother was one of the people who wrote it!
For years people have thought this was my composition because I do

148

write so much of what I record. But this song was written by Orville Couch and Bobbie Jean Carroll. I never met either one of them, nor have I ever heard the story of how they came to compose this incredibly important song in my career. Orville Couch passed away a few years ago, and I've never known who Bobbie Jean Carroll was or how to get in touch with her. And now...after all these years...she's coming to meet me and hear me sing her song on stage at the Ryman Auditorium in just a few days.

How incredibly cool is THAT?

Just when you think you've seen and heard it all in this business, things like this seem to drop right out of the sky. Do you reckon God really DOES like country music? I have to believe He does.

Roy Acuff

November 20, 2006

Hi Gang:

For the past several Thanksgiving seasons, I have written in this space that one of my boyhood heroes was a sportswriter in Atlanta named Furman Bisher. When I was a teenager and attempting to be a bit of a sportswriter myself, I wanted to grow up to be him.

Every Thanksgiving he would (and still does so far as I know) write a column in the Atlanta Journal-Constitution listing the things he was most thankful for that particular year. With apologies to him once again for borrowing his idea, I've made another list of my own:

I'M THANKFUL….

For the sun that came up this morning over the Tennessee hills, and that I was able to get out of bed, make coffee, and be gifted with another day as a small part of God's incredible creation.

For my three children, their spouses, and my six grandchildren, all of whom are now back home and living in the greater Nashville area. I realized how much I had missed them one recent afternoon when I wasn't feeling well. My daughter, Jenni, came to the door with a big bowl of her homemade potato soup. I nicknamed it my "hillbilly penicillin!"

I'm thankful that almost a half-century after having written my first #1 hit song I was able to get together with some co-writing buddies of mine and do it again. And I'm thankful for George Strait and his incredible rendition of that song, "Give It Away." And I'm thankful that in this day of complicated melodies and rocking rhythm patterns in country music, our song was simply three-chords and the truth.

I'm thankful for 45-years as a performing member of the Grand Ole Opry. And I'm especially thankful for the celebration my fan club staged in my honor this past July when I reached that milestone.

I'm thankful for having had a "little sister" in my life ever since I was four-and-a-half years old, and I'm so proud of the long, courageous fight she put up against cancer. And I'm especially thankful that, in the last years of her life, she and I were able to come to the realization that the things we had in common were so much stronger than any differences that might have ever existed between us. Thanksgiving and Christmas were her two favorite days of the year. I'll miss sharing them with her this year…and every year until we can be together again.

I'm thankful for the little lady I met this summer working behind the counter at the donut shop in Maine. I walked in to order a glass of orange juice and she said, "You look like a singer that I used to like." I tried to keep a straight face and asked her his name. "Bill Anderson," she replied. "You don't like him anymore?" I inquired. "No," she said, he hasn't put out anything good in a long time." Then, as it slowly began to dawn on her that I just might be the singer she was talking about, she quickly added, "But my mother still likes him a lot!"

And I'm thankful for the memories of Thanksgivings past...the smell of mama's turkey and dressing hot from the oven and the heartfelt blessing my daddy would always offer prior to the meal. Nobody before or since could offer thanks to the Lord for our "many, many blessings" quite like my daddy.

I'm thankful that I'll have all my children, their spouses, and all my grandchildren at my house this Thanksgiving Day. I hope I can help create some special memories for them the way my folks always did for me.

I continue to be thankful every day for our servicemen and women who, by no choice of their own, must spend Thanksgiving apart from their loved ones this year because they are somewhere helping to preserve and protect the freedoms the rest of us too often take for granted.

I'm thankful for the man up in Ohio who found the old acetate recording of mine in a pile of vintage records he purchased at a yard sale or flea market. It was a political jingle I had written and sung for our incumbent congressman when I was 15 or 16 years old. He took the scratchy old recording and, with modern technology, made it sound new. He went to a lot of trouble to share it with me. Someday, I hope I can share it with you.

I'm even thankful for the lady who recently read my autobiography and, after subjecting herself to four-hundred-plus pages of all that I had done in my busy life, wrote and asked, "When did you have time to go potty?"

And I'm thankful to each of you, my fans and my friends, who took the time to stop by my web site today. I have often said that I don't have the most fans in country music, but I sure have some of the very best! May we each be renewed by the season and reminded once again of our "many, many blessings"....not just at Thanksgiving, but on every single day of the year.

November 27, 2006

Hi Gang:

Well, it's my favorite time of year again…of course, I'm talking about Christmas.

Oh, I've got so many great memories of Christmases in my life…everybody gathering at our house…grandparents, aunts, uncles, and cousins..

Going with my daddy to pick out a Christmas tree for the whole family to decorate...

I once even played the part of a shepherd in a Christmas play at church…

Oh, and I still remember how hard it was to go to sleep on Christmas Eve knowing that Santa was on his way.

But, you know, things have changed a lot down through the years. And somewhere along the way, I think maybe the world just got in too big of a hurry. I first began to notice it when people started writing Xmas instead of Christmas.

And now some people want to call Christmas the "winter break" or the "winter holiday." And that's sad to me, 'cause it seems like folks are even afraid to say the word "Christmas" anymore.

Well, the first word in Christmas is "Christ"…and it's His birthday that those of us who call ourselves Christians celebrate every December the 25th.

I wouldn't dare try to tell anyone else that they couldn't celebrate the holiday of THEIR faith any way they might see fit. The last time I checked, this was still the land of the free. And that means that I'm free to celebrate Christmas for what it means to me.

So, I'm gonna go out this year and I'm gonna buy CHRISTMAS presents…and I'm gonna send my friends CHRISTMAS cards…and sing CHRISTMAS carols…and eat CHRISTMAS cookies…and tell the CHRISTMAS story to my kids and my grandkids…and anybody else that might care to listen.

O.K.…call me "politically incorrect" if you want to. I've been called a lot worse things in my life.

I've seen a lot of Christmases come and go down through the years, and I'm looking forward to this one…and the next one and the next one. So,

allow me to say to you and yours, "Merry CHRISTMAS"...
Because even after all this time...in fact, maybe now even more than
ever...I am still believing in CHRISTMAS! *

* "Still Believing In Christmas"
  Words & Music by Bill Anderson & Dave Lindsey
  Mr. Bubba Music, Inc./Sony-ATV Publishing - BMI
  Dave Lindsey Music - ASCAP
  Copyright 2006

I got a letter from a fan in 2006 who told me he had last seen me in concert in 1973.

"You remember me, I'm sure," he wrote. "I had a green hat and a pink shirt."

Grandpa Jones while trying to tune his banjo: "I don't hate but two things. Hitler and B-strings."

Somebody once asked Merle Haggard why he wrote "Okie From Muskogee." Hag thought awhile then answered, "Because I'm the only one who knew the words."

Most audiences love to hear fiddle players play "The Orange Blossom Special." Most fiddle players, on the other hand, don't like to play it. One of the greatest, Johnny Gimble, once said, "If I ever get Alzheimer's, the first thing I'm going to forget is the Orange Blossom Special."

Roger Miller said his hometown was so small they didn't even have a town drunk. So they all took turns.

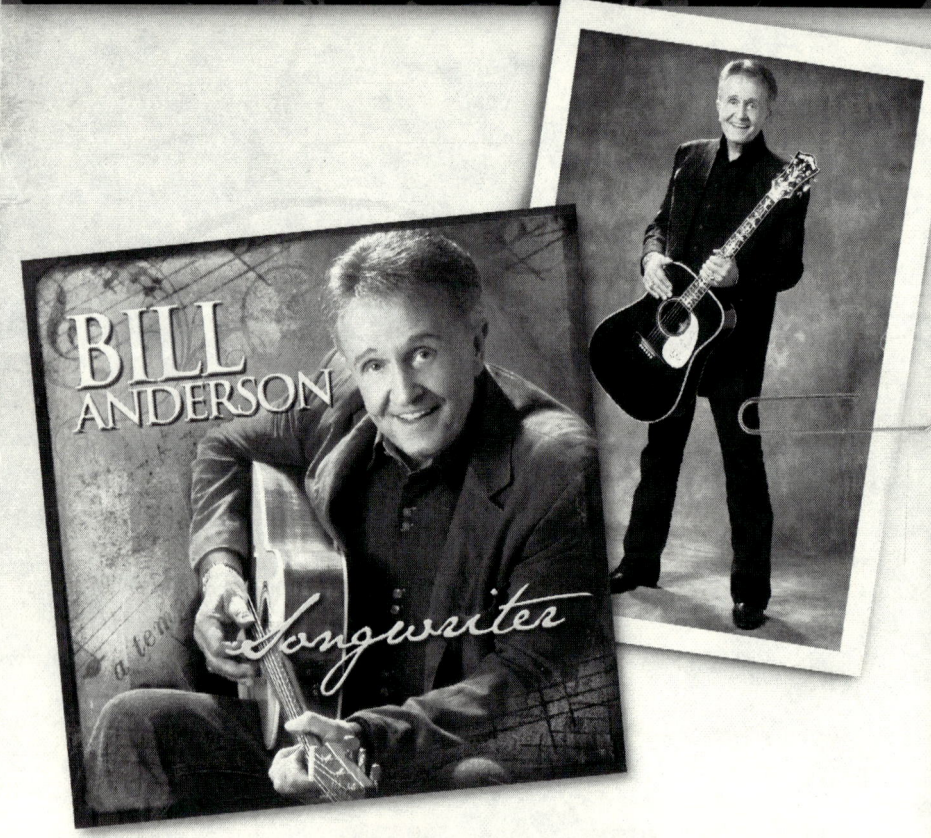

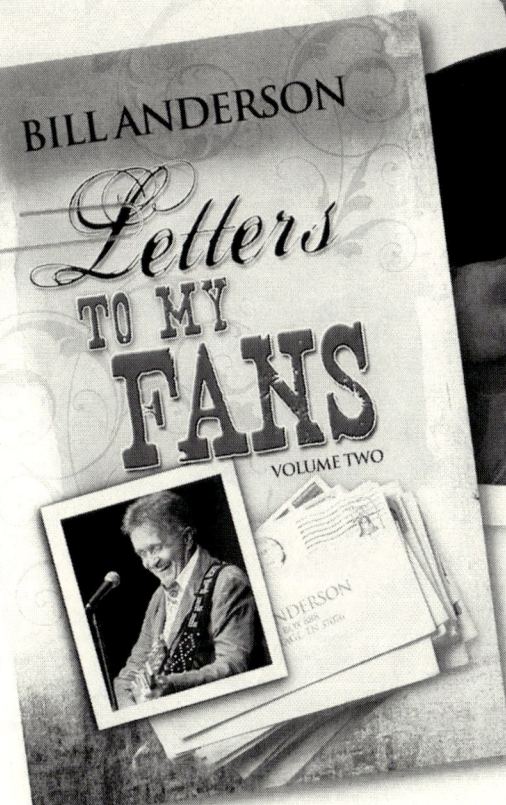